Library of
Davidson College

VOID

Garland English Texts

Stephen Orgel
Editor

Jerome McGann
Associate Editor

THE
Lamentable Tragedie of

Locrine, the eldest sonne of King *Brutus*, discoursing the warres of the *Britaines*, and *Hunnes*, with their discomfiture:

The Britaines *victorie with their Accidents, and the death of* Albanact. *No lesse pleasant then profitable.*

Newly set foorth, ouerseene and corrected,
By *W. S.*

LONDON
Printed by Thomas Creede.
1595.

Reproduced by permission of The Huntington Library, San Marino, California

The Lamentable Tragedy of Locrine
A Critical Edition

edited by
Jane Lytton Gooch

Garland English Texts
Number 7

GARLAND PUBLISHING, INC.
NEW YORK & LONDON
1981

Copyright © 1981 by Jane Lytton Gooch
All rights reserved

Library of Congress Cataloging in Publication Data

Locrine.
  The lamentable tragedy of Locrine.

  (Garland English texts ; no. 7)
  Based on the 1595 quarto, this ed. is a revision of the editor's thesis (Ph. D.)—University of Toronto.
  Original work has been attributed to Shakespeare (included in the 3rd (1664) and 4th (1685) folios), William Smith, et al.
  Bibliography: p.
  Includes index.
  I. Gooch, Jane Lytton. II. Shakespeare, William, 1564–1616. III. Smith, William, fl. 1596. IV. Title. V. Series.
PR2862.A114   1981   822'.3   80-8986
ISBN 0-8240-9407-7   AACR2

Printed on acid-free, 250-year-life paper
Manufactured in the United States of America

Contents

PREFACE	vii
ABBREVIATIONS	ix
INTRODUCTION	
1. Sources	1
2. Date	4
3. Structure	10
4. Historical Themes	20
5. Authorship	27
6. Attribution to Company	32
7. Text	34
THE LAMENTABLE TRAGEDY OF LOCRINE	39
APPENDICES	
A. *The Mirror for Magistrates:* "Albanact," ll.414-518	139
B. *The Complaint of Elstred*, ll.181-222, 409-432	142
C. Comparison of *Selimus* (ll.414-416, 2422-2429), *Locrine* (II,vi,1-17), and "Ruines of Rome" (ll.149-166)	144
BIBLIOGRAPHY	147
GLOSSARIAL INDEX TO THE COMMENTARY	167

Preface

This edition of *The Lamentable Tragedy of Locrine* is based on the thirteen copies of the 1595 quarto, and no copies show any press variants; the modernized text includes a critical introduction, textual notes and commentary, appendices, a glossary, and a full bibliography. All works cited in the introduction, textual notes, and commentary are found in the bibliography. Most titles are given first with full details and subsequently appear in a shortened form. Some abbreviations of standard reference works and editions of *Locrine* have been used for convenience throughout the introduction, commentary, and textual notes; these abbreviations are listed immediately following the Preface.

I should like to express my gratitude for the assistance offered by the following libraries: for access to the 1595 quarto of *Locrine*, the British Library, the library of Trinity College, Cambridge, the Bodleian Library, the Folger Shakespeare Library, the Pierpont Morgan Library; for supplying microfilm of the 1595 quarto, the preceding libraries and the Birmingham Public Library, the University of Illinois Library, the Henry Huntington Library, the Clark Library; for permission to use a photograph of the title page of the 1595 quarto, the Henry Huntington Library; and for use of the library collection and reference facilities, the British Library, the Folger Shakespeare Library, the University of Toronto Library, and the University of British Columbia Library.

This edition began as a doctoral dissertation at the University of Toronto, and I should like to offer my special thanks to A.C. Lancashire, J.L. Levenson and R.E. Fantham for their help in the early stages of my work; to G.R. Proudfoot for sharing with me the result of his collation of the quarto copies of *Locrine* (prepared for an edition of the Shakespeare Apocrypha) - especially the copy in the Bibliotheca Bodmeriana (Cologny, Geneva) for which microfilm was unavailable; to my parents, Mr. and Mrs. K.G. Tryon, for their years of support; to the supervisor of my dissertation, S.P. Zitner, for his constant help and encouragement; to my husband, Bryan N.S. Gooch, for his generous assistance throughout the various stages of the dissertation and the revision for publication; and, finally, to the General Editor, Stephen Orgel, who has given me much valuable advice, particularly in the dating of the play.

JANE LYTTON GOOCH

Vancouver, 1980

Abbreviations

(A) WORKS OF REFERENCE

Abbott
: E.A. Abbott, *A Shakespearian Grammar*, 1870, rpt. 1966.

Arber
: Edward Arber, ed., *Transcript of the Registers of the Company of Stationers of London 1554-1640 A.D.*, 1875-1894.

Cooper
: Thomas Cooper, *Thesaurus Linguae Romanae et Britannicae*, 1565.

Historia
: Geoffrey of Monmouth, *Historia Regum Britanniae*, 1139.

Onions
: C.T. Onions, *A Shakespeare Glossary*, 1911.

O.C.D.
: *Oxford Classical Dictionary.*

O.E.D.
: *Oxford English Dictionary.*

Tilley
: M.P. Tilley, *A Dictionary of the Proverbs in England in the Sixteenth and Seventeenth Centuries*, 1950.

(B) EDITIONS CITED IN THE NOTES

Q
: *The Lamentable Tragedy of Locrine*, 1595.

F
: *Mr. William Shakespeare's Comedies, Histories and Tragedies*, 1664.

F2
: *Mr. William Shakespeare's Comedies, Histories and Tragedies*, 1685.

Rowe
: *The Works of Mr. William Shakspear*, ed. Nicholas Rowe, 1709, Vol. 6.

Pope
: *The Works of Shakespear*, ed. Alexander Pope, 1728, Vol. 9.

M	*Supplement to the Edition of Shakespear's Plays Published in 1778 by S. Johnson and G. Steevens ...With Notes by the Editor and Others*, ed. Edmund Malone, 1780, Vol. 2.
Steevens	George Steevens, notes included in the *Supplement*, ed. Edmund Malone, 1780, Vol. 2.
Th	Lewis Theobald, notes included in the *Supplement*, ed. Edmund Malone, 1780, Vol. 2.
Simms	*A Supplement to the Plays*, ed. W.G. Simms, 1848.
Tyrrell	*The Doubtful Plays of Shakespeare*, ed. Henry Tyrrell, 1851.
Hazlitt	*The Supplementary Works of William Shakspeare*, ed. William Hazlitt, 1852.
Moltke	*Doubtful Plays of Wm. Shakespeare*, ed. Max Moltke, 1869.
McKerrow	*The Tragedy of Locrine 1595*, ed. Ronald B. McKerrow, 1908 (Malone Society Reprints).
Brooke	*The Shakespeare Apocrypha*, ed. C.F. Tucker Brooke, 1908.

Quotations and line-numbers for Shakespeare are from W.J. Craig's one-volume Oxford edition (1943). Abbreviations for the titles of Shakespeare's plays are taken from C.T. Onions, *A Shakespeare Glossary* (1911), p. x.

INTRODUCTION

1. SOURCES

The primary source for *The Lamentable Tragedy of Locrine* is the twelfth century chronicle by Geoffrey of Monmouth, the *Historia Regum Britanniae*. The *Historia* traces the heroic beginnings of the British people from the time of the Trojan war: Brutus, a direct descendant of Aeneas, is able to liberate his fellow Trojans from Greek captivity; after a long voyage, directed by the prophecy of Venus, and a fierce battle with the French army of Tours, Brutus and his followers establish the colony of Troynovant, New Troy, at the mouth of the Thames. The noble lineage traced from the Trojan heroes, the quest for a homeland, the great deeds of valour in battle, including the expulsion of a race of giants from the island, all lend an atmosphere of the legendary. Although Geoffrey gives his chronicle the appearance of historical authenticity, by claiming in the epistle dedicatory that he had merely translated into Latin an old book written in the British tongue which was in the possession of Walter, Archdeacon of Oxford, any factural material that the narrative may contain has been enriched with his own invention.

A comprehensive comparison of all accounts of the Locrine story by Theodor Erbe leads to the conclusion that all versions have a remarkable similarity, differing from one another only in details.[1] Three poems contemporary with *Locrine*--*The Mirror For Magistrates*, *The Complaint of Elstred*, and *The Faerie Queene*--have contributed significant details of plot and character to the play. The main organization of the material, however, comes from the *Historia*. The background information concerning the life of Brutus has been condensed into Brutus' dying speech, and the principal events of Locrine's reign, the defeat of the barbarian invaders and Locrine's love for Estrild, follow the chronology of the

[1]"Die Locrinesage und die Quellen des pseudo-shakespeareschen *Locrine*," *Studien zur englischen Philologie*, 16 (1904), 1-73. Erbe also notes that several minor characters in *Locrine*--Hubba, Segar, Trussier and Thrasimachus--are not found in any source (p. 65).

Historia. The patriotic and legendary character of Geoffrey's chronicle is carried over into the play, in the report of Brutus' exploits and in the episodes concerned with the naming of the Humber and Severn rivers. One important invention of the dramatist is the suicides of four of the main characters: Albanact, Locrine, Estrild, and Sabren.[2] In the *Historia* Locrine and Albanact are killed in battle, and both Estrild and Sabren are drowned by Guendoline. As Wolfgang Clemen points out in his discussion of the dramatic lament, the source material has been adapted to allow frequent opportunities for the rhetorical flourishes of the lament preceding a character's death.[3] Humber's life, in fact, is prolonged after his defeat, apparently for seven years, in order to allow for three laments before he finally drowns himself.[4]

John Higgins added to *The Mirror For Magistrates* in order to complete the span of British history begun by Baldwin; the additions include the five complaints of Albanact, Humber, Locrinus, Elstride and Sabren. The first scene in *Locrine*, after the dumb show, appears to have been influenced directly by Higgins' "Complaint of Albanact." The sequence of thought in the speech of Brutus as he is dying is similar in the play and the complaint:[5] after reviewing his past exploits with the hope that all his efforts have not been in vain, Brutus makes a last request to his nobles to give his sons good counsel; he divides the kingdom and instructs his sons to heed the advice of their counsellors and maintain concord among themselves. After his death, there are similarities in the lamentations, the expression of the inevitability of death and the plans to bury Brutus at Troynovant.[6]

A poem in the "Mirror" tradition that probably influenced *Locrine* is *The Complaint of Elstred* by Thomas

[2]*Ibid.*, p. 70.
[3]*English Tragedy Before Shakespeare*, trans. T.S. Dorsch (London: Methuen, 1961), p. 260.
[4]The Humber plot gives evidence of a revision in the play's structure; see Introduction, p. 9.
[5]For a detailed comparison of the *Mirror* and the play at this point, see Baldwin Maxwell, *Studies in the Shakespeare Apocrypha* (New York: King's Crown Press, 1956), pp. 27-32. See Appendix A for the relevant passage from the *Mirror*.
[6]Farnham notes ("John Higgins' *Mirror* and *Locrine*," *Modern Philology*, 23 (1925-26), 308) that Brutus' reference to the death of his nephew, Turnus, in *Locrine*, "And for your sakes my Turnus there I lost" (I,ii,113), is similar to the concept of sacrifice in the "Complaint of Albanact"--"Where you to saue I loste my faithful frende" (1.426).

Lodge.⁷ Baldwin Maxwell has done a thorough comparison of the *Complaint* and *Locrine*, and he observes that two scenes in the play, the first meeting between Locrine and Estrild and Estrild's lament over Locrine's corpse, are not found in any other account except the *Complaint*. When Elstrid makes her first appearance in the play (IV,ii), she laments her fate in a thirty-line speech organized into five stanzas rhyming ababcc; this extensive rhyme scheme, a sudden departure from the limited use of rhyme in the rest of the play, is found throughout the *Complaint*.⁸ In the play, Locrine and Estrild complain of their unhappy fates, one a prisoner of war and the other a prisoner of love; their complaints are complementary and the final lines of each combine to form an elaborate stanza of rhyming stichomythia:

> Est. Hard is their fall, who from a golden crown
>   Are cast into a sea of wretchedness.
> Loc. [Aside] Hard is their thrall, who by Cupid's frown
>   Are wrapped in waves of endless carefulness.
> Est. O kingdom, object to all miseries.
> Loc. [Aside] O love, the extrem'st of all extremities. (IV,ii, 103-108)

This formal rhetorical structure seems more appropriate to the genre of Lodge's poem, the complaint, than to the drama. The sudden increase in stylization which occurs at this point in *Locrine* probably reflects the dramatist's imitation of his source.⁹

The early history of Britain is given in another apparent source, *The Faerie Queene*, in two parts: Book II, Canto x, when Sir Guyon reads from "An auncient booke, hight *Briton moniments*" (II,ix,59), beginning with the arrival of Brutus and continuing with the succession of kings to the time of Uther Pendragon; and Book III, Canto ix, when Britomart traces her Trojan ancestry from the time of the Trojan war through the life of Brutus to the founding of Troynovant. Significant details in this account of Britain's origins appear to have influenced

---

⁷John Tatlock (*The Legendary History of Britain* (Berkeley: University of California Press, 1950), p. 128) points out that the principal source of all accounts of the Elstrid story, including that in the *Historia*, is William of Malmesbury's *Gesta Pontificum* (1125).

⁸*Shakespeare Apocrypha*, pp. 33-38. See Appendix B for the relevant passages in *The Complaint of Elstred*.

⁹Another borrowing, which strengthens the association with Lodge, is the use in Humber's lament of the Latin line "*O vita misero longa, foelici brevis!*" (IV,v,1), which is the motto on the title-page of *The Wounds of Civil War* (1594).

Locrine. In the story of the battle with the giants, Spenser mentions Debon along with Corineus as having subdued one of the giants. As a reward for his valour Debon was given Devonshire just as Corineus was awarded Cornwall. Debon does not appear in any other source material except *The Faerie Queene*, and although he plays a minor role in *Locrine*, he has been carefully interwoven into the texture of the drama.[10] The name of Trompart, the clown's man in *Locrine*, has also been borrowed from *The Faerie Queene*.[11] In Spenser's poem Trompart is a squire to Braggadocchio (II,iii,10), and his function, as his name suggests, is to go before the braggart soldier extolling his praises. One of the roles that Strumbo assumes is that of the braggart soldier, and thus Trompart takes not only his name but also his character from *The Faerie Queene*. When Strumbo and Trompart are involved in the battle against Humber in Act II, the comic subplot is closely tied to the serious plot. The evidence of two minor characters with Spenserian names, Debon and Trompart, who are integrated with the rest of the play suggests the completion or revision of *Locrine* after the author had read *The Faerie Queene*.

With *The Faerie Queene* established as a source, it seems reasonable to suppose that the author of *Locrine* also borrowed a significant detail of plot, Locrine's marriage to Guendoline before he meets Estrild.[12] In the *Historia*, Locrine is forced to fulfil his promise to Guendoline and marry her only after he has met and fallen in love with Estrild. Although several other accounts of Locrine's reign agree with *The Faerie Queene* and the play with respect to his marriage, namely Warner's *Albion's England* and the chronicles of Rastell, Fabyan, and Grafton, the author of *Locrine* seems to have worked primarily with Spenser's poem.

2. DATE

On the basis of evidence afforded by the title-page and the epilogue, the latest date possible for *Locrine* is 1595. The title-page states that *Locrine* was printed by Thomas Creede in 1595. The last speech in the play

---

[10]Carrie A. Harper ("'Locrine' and the 'Faerie Queene'," *Modern Language Review*, 8 (1913), 369-71) notes that although Debon speaks only four lines (I,ii,139-40; II,iv,17-18), he is mentioned in the stage direction as having been killed in the battle with the Huns (II,vi,27.2), and he is referred to as a fallen hero in two other instances (II,vi,65 and III,ii,35-36).

[11]This was first observed by Sir Aldolphus W. Ward, *History of English Dramatic Literature to the Death of Queen Anne* (London: Macmillan, 1899), II,221.

[12]Erbe, "Die Locrinesage," p. 71.

INTRODUCTION   5

contains a prayer for Elizabeth, "That eight and thirty
years the scepter swayed" (V,vi,203). The thirty-eighth
regnal year extended from November 17, 1595 to November
16, 1596, thus placing the printing of *Locrine* late in
1595. The play was probably completed in its final form,
perhaps with the exception of the epilogue, by July 20,
1594, the date of entry in the Stationers' Register:

                      die Iulij 1594

Entred for his Copie vnder th[e h]andes of   Thomas Creede
the Wardens. *The lamentable Tragedie of*
LOCRINE, the eldest sonne of Kinge BRUTUS.
discoursinge the warres of the Brittans
&c. . . vj^d
                         (Arber, II, 656)

  The earliest date suggested for *Locrine* is 1585, by
McKerrow in his Malone Society Reprint (p.vi): "...the
date of composition probably preceded that of publication
by almost a decade." Tucker Brooke, in *The Shakespeare
Apocrypha* (p. xx), strongly supports this opinion:
"*Locrine* is a tragedy of the type of about 1585; that it
could have been composed--with all its dumb show
machinery and so forth--immediately before 1595 is
practically impossible." McKerrow and Tucker Brooke are
basing their opinions on the academic nature of *Locrine*.
the long declamatory speeches and the dumb shows preceding each act, characteristic of a type of tragedy written
for the Inns of Court.[13] Certainly by 1580 this academic
tragedy had given way to a more realistic type of drama,
but it is possible that a lesser dramatist might continue
to use techniques that had proven successful. One piece
of evidence that supports a date of composition about
1585 is a manuscript note on one of the quarto copies of
Locrine (now in the Bibliotheca Bodmeriana, Cologny,
Geneva), apparently in the hand of George Buc, Master of
the Revels, which ascribes the play to Charles Tilney,
who was executed for treason in 1586. W. W. Greg has
transcribed and reconstructed the note as follows:

---

[13]Typical examples include *Gordobuc* (1561), *Jocasta* (1566),
Gismund of Salerne (1568; revised for publication as *Tancred and
Gismund* in 1591), *The Misfortunes of Arthur* (1587); see C.F. Tucker
Brooke, *The Tudor Drama* (Boston: Houghton Mifflin, 1911),
pp. 188-229.

```
Char. Tilney wrote ⟨a⟩  ⟨ch⟩
Tragedy of this mattr ⟨w  ⟩
hee named Estrild: ⟨&wch⟩ J think is this. it was l⟨ost?⟩
by his death. & now[?] 's ⟨ome?⟩ fellow hath published ⟨it.⟩
J made dūbe shewes for it.
wch J yet haue. G.B⟨.⟩¹⁴
```

The note was first discovered by John Payne Collier and his reputation for forgery immediately surrounded the ascription with suspicion. He claims that the handwriting on the copy of *Locrine* is similar to that of an inscription to Lord Ellesmere in a copy of Buc's "Eclog."[15] This evidence is, at once, misleading because the two specimens of writing are obviously dissimilar. As Marc Eccles points out, the inscription to Ellesmere is written in Buc's formal Italian hand.[16] Greg sees such a close similarity between Buc's handwriting and the notes in *Locrine* and *George-a-Green* that he doubts whether a forger could have reproduced the individual character of Buc's writing, particularly his habit of touching up his letters.[17] On the other hand, Samuel A. Tannenbaum rejects the authenticity of the note in *Locrine* for the same reason: he claims that the letters were constructed piece by piece and that the writing was done in a slow, unsteady fashion.[18] R. C. Bald supports Greg; after comparing one of Buc's manuscripts, "A Commentary upon the New Roulle of Winchester," with the title-page inscriptions in *Locrine* and *George-a-Green*, he concludes that both notes are genuine and show the characteristic of Buc for "Retouchings, rewritings, erasures, erased passages overwritten..."[19] Assuming the note to be genuine, and the weight of evidence

[14]"Three Manuscript Notes by Sir George Buc," *Library*, 4th ser., 12 (1932), 314. See Plate II for a photographic reproduction of Buc's note.

[15]*A Bibliographical and Critical Account of the Rarest Books in the English Language* (London: Joseph Lilly, 1865), I,95: "A comparison with this specimen of the Penmanship of the Master of the Revels [Ellesmere inscription] leaves no doubt that the inscription on an existing copy of the play of *Locrine*, 4to. 1595, assigning the authorship of it to Charles Tylney, is the handwriting of Sir George Buck."

[16]"Sir George Buc, Master of the Revels," *Thomas Lodge and Other Elizabethans*, ed. Charles J. Sisson (New York: Octagon Books, 1966), pp. 438, 455; two other examples of this formal script are available in another inscribed copy of the "Eclog" to the Earl of Northampton and in the dedication of Buc's *History of the Life and Reign of Richard the Third*.

[17]"Three Manuscript Notes," pp. 315-316.

[18]*Shaksperian Scraps and Other Elizabethan Fragments* (New York: Columbia University Press, 1933), p. 70.

[19]"The *Locrine* and *George-a-Greene* Title-Page Inscriptions," *Library*, 4th ser., 15 (1935), 305.

appears convincing, there is still, as T. W. Baldwin remarks, an element of conjecture in Buc's statement: he is not sure that *Locrine* is the same play that Tilney wrote under the name of *Estrild*, even though he made the dumb shows for Tilney's play.[20] At least two of the dumb shows, those concerning the lion and the crocodile, appear to have been borrowed directly from Spenser's *Complaints*. The *Complaints* were not published until 1591, but according to the Preface by the printer, they were old poems "disperst abroad in sundrie hands,"[21] and Buc may have had access to them in manuscript five years before the actual date of publication. The other three dumb shows, based on classical stories about love and marriage and suited to a play about Estrild, may have been part of Tilney's play which were incorporated into another version of the story, *Locrine*.

Locrine contains numerous borrowings from contemporary poetry and drama, published in the period 1590-1594. Some or all of these works may have been available to the author or reviser of *Locrine* in manuscript, and, thus, the earliest possible date of composition or of subsequent revisions is difficult to determine exactly. *The Faerie Queene*, the first three books of which were published in 1590, has been shown to be a source for *Locrine* in both the serious and comic plots.[22] The borrowings from the *Complaints*, entered in the Stationers' Register on December 29, 1590 (Arber,II,570) and printed in 1591, are confined generally to the first half of the play, the plot concerning Albanact: the commentary with the dumb shows at the beginning of Acts I and III; Brutus' dying speech (I,ii); Humber's speech in the midst of battle (II,vi); Locrine's lament on the death of Albanact (III,ii). The one exception is a line adapted from the "Teares of the Muses" (157), "That all our life is but a Tragedie," in Ate's speech (III,i), which is repeated by Estrild (V,vi). When all of the explicit borrowings from Spenser are considered together--Locrine's marriage, the characters of Debon and Trompart, the lines from the *Complaints*--we see that they all come from the first half of the play. Trompart makes his last appearance as Strumbo's man in III,iv, but he does not speak nor does he appear to take part in the action. Apparently, the first part of *Locrine* was written or rewritten under Spenser's influence.

[20]*On The Literary Genetics of Shakspere's Plays 1592-1594* (Urbana: University of Illinois Press, 1959), p. 218.
[21]Edmund Spenser, *Poetical Works*, ed. J. C. Smith and E. De Selincourt (London: Oxford University Press, 1912), p. 470.
[22]The clown, Strumbo, in his first monologue on the tribulations of love (I,iii), borrows a line from Spenser's knight Pyrochles-- "I burne, I burne, I burne" (II,vi,44).

Thomas Lodge's *The Complaint of Elstred*, a probable source for *Locrine*, was not published until 1593, although it is possible that it was available in manuscript before then. The sudden intrusion of an elaborate rhyme scheme into the play, on the first appearance of Estrild, suggests that this particular scene was a later insertion, perhaps after the Spenserian borrowings had been incorporated into the play. In any case, the borrowings from Spenser and Lodge are found in separate parts of *Locrine*, each connected with one of the major actions of the play.

Locrine bears a special relationship to *The Tragical Reign of Selimus*, printed by Thomas Creede in 1594. The similarities are so numerous, extending to whole passages, that the date of *Locrine* cannot be determined without first knowing the date of *Selimus*. *Locrine* was entered in the Stationers' Register on July 20, 1594; *Selimus* was published the same year but without a previous entry in the Stationers' Register. *Selimus* borrows from Sidney's *Arcadia*[23] (printed 1590) and from Spenser's *Faerie Queene*[24] and *Complaints*. An interesting verbal parallel occurs between *Selimus* (11.945-47) and Kyd's *Cornelia* (IV,i,63-65). Kyd states in the preface that he prepared his translation in the winter of 1593-94 and, thus, if the author or reviser of *Selimus* borrowed from *Cornelia*, *Selimus* was completed in its final form early in 1594.[25]

Both *Locrine* and *Selimus* borrow from the same passage in the "Ruines of Rome"; the borrowing in *Locrine* is confined to one passage whereas the lines in *Selimus* appear in two widely separated passages. This indicates that the direction of borrowing is from Spenser to *Locrine* and, subsequently, to *Selimus*, where the original passage is divided. The reverse process of taking two separate passages from *Selimus* and combining them in *Locrine* seems more difficult, and, therefore, less likely.[26]

Other similarities between *Locrine* and *Selimus*, besides numerous verbal parallels, include a stanzaic rhyme scheme (ababcc), a characteristic type of stage direction, and a comic scene. Throughout *Selimus* there

---

[23] Baldwin, *Literary Genetics*, p. 224.

[24] See Charles Crawford, "Edmund Spenser, 'Locrine' and 'Selimus'," *Notes & Queries*, 9th ser., 7 (1901), 142-43, 203-4, 261, for parallels between *The Faerie Queene* and *Selimus*.

[25] Matthew P. McDiarmid, "The Influence of Robert Garnier on Some Elizabethan Tragedies," *Etudes Anglaises*, 11 (1958), 298.

[26] Frank G. Hubbard discusses the relationship between the two plays in "*Locrine* and *Selimus*," *Shakespeare Studies* by Members of the Department of English in The University of Wisconsin (Madison: University of Wisconsin Press, 1916), pp. 17-35. See Appendix C for the relevant passages from the plays and "Ruines of Rome."

are seven stanzas rhyming ababcc; this particular six-line stanza is found in *Locrine* only in the scene in which Locrine first meets Estrild. Most stage directions in *Selimus* consist of a list of characters' names without any descriptive detail, but in several instances this pattern is varied, for example "*Acomat* must read a letter, and then renting it say:" (xi). In the dumb shows and both the comic and serious plots of *Locrine* this type of stage direction, which concludes with "saying," appears several times, for example "Enter HUMBER alone, saying" (IV,v). The stage directions for the comic scenes in both *Selimus* and *Locrine* give evidence of the author's hand in their specific descriptions of attitude and appearance.[27] Comedy in *Selimus* is limited to one scene with the clown, Bullithrumble, and a brief appearance by him after this initial scene. The Bullithrumble episode shows a marked similarity with the encounter between Humber and Strumbo, both in the verbal parallels and in the basic situation--the clown, after soliloquizing on the tribulations of married life, proceeds to eat a meal when he is approached by a hungry fugitive. The source material for *Selimus*, as Baldwin Maxwell points out in his discussion of the relationship of the two plays in *Studies in the Shakespeare Apocrypha* (pp. 56-63), leads naturally to the meeting between the fugitive Corcut and the clown Bullithrumble; this meeting, also, serves an important function in furthering the action, as it results in the betrayal of Corcut's shepherd disguise. In *Locrine*, however, the encounter between Strumbo and Humber does not come from source material nor is it prepared for by the rest of the play; the action does not progress as a result, except that Humber's misery and lamentations are prolonged for seven years without the knowledge of the other characters in the play, and the scene allows for the introduction of two popular characters, the clown and the ghost. On the basis of the evidence in both plays, it seems probable that *Selimus* borrowed the lines in the *Complaints* from *Locrine*, but, on the other hand, *Locrine* borrowed the Bullithrumble scene from *Selimus*. The reviser of *Locrine* could not have extracted the Bullithrumble scene from *Selimus* and adapted it to his play later than 1594 when *Selimus* was published and *Locrine* was entered in the Stationers' Register.

Certainly the style of *Locrine* suggests a date of composition of about 1585 as McKerrow has pointed out. The Buc note about Charles Tilney supports this early date. The play, however, has been markedly influenced by *The Faerie Queene*, the *Complaints*, *The Complaint of Elstred*, and *Selimus*, all of which appeared in printed

---

[27]Baldwin Maxwell compares the stage directions in both plays (*Shakespeare Apocrypha*, pp. 51-52, 69-70); for a further discussion of stage directions in *Locrine* see Introduction, p. 36.

form between 1590 and 1594. All may have been available to one or more revisers of *Locrine* in manuscript some years prior to their date of publication. The available evidence suggests that *Locrine* was first written around 1585 and then went through several stages of revision, perhaps by a number of different hands, until it was completed in its final form in 1594 and entered in the Stationers' Register.

3. STRUCTURE

In *Locrine* legendary history, pageantry and comedy have been moulded together into a play designed to entertain a popular audience. The main plot, based on early British history, not only exploits the patriotic appeal of a victorious British army but also the romantic appeal of a sentimental love affair involving the king. The themes of the tragic action are repeated in the dumb shows and the comic episodes: both frame the main plot, the dumb shows emphasizing the serious moral message of the play, through mythological story and beast fable presented and explained by the goddess Ate, and the lighter scenes undercutting the themes of love and war with a comic presenter in the person of Strumbo, a character at home in contemporary London.

The three levels of the play, dumb show, tragedy and comedy, are integrated through a common concern for the principal ideas of love and war. These ideas, however, are expressed by means of such different dramatic techniques on each level of the play that we have the impression of three plays rolled into one. The relation of speech to action, for example, is different in each of the dramatic spheres: in the dumb shows speech and action are completely separate; in the serious main plot, long set speeches are juxtaposed with furious battles; and in the comic subplot an integration is achieved between monologue and stage business. The dumb shows introduce each act with the spectacle of the pageants; the silent picture followed by an explanation reveals an affinity with the emblem books. The tragic plot presents a series of battles linked by the motif of revenge; in contrast to the activity of battle are the long set speeches, particularly laments, during which action comes to a standstill while a character philosophizes on the outcome of one of the battles. The comic subplot presents a number of separate episodes unified through the person of the clown; by showing Strumbo as a soldier and a lover, these episodes parody the heroic and romantic assumptions of the serious main plot, both in theme and language.

The dumb shows provide silent action, followed by choric commentary, before each act in *Locrine*, and thus supply a formal regularity to the structure of the play. A typical construction for the popular play based on chronicle history may be seen in *Edward I* or *The Famous*

Victories, where scenes follow one another consecutively without a division into acts. The dumb shows in *Locrine*, which departs from such a pattern, reflect the influence of Senecan models in which the drama was regularly divided by the chorus. On the other hand, as Dieter Mehl suggests,[28] the classical regimen was not congenial to Elizabethan dramatists because even when the imitation of Senecan form was the closest, as in *Gorboduc*, action was introduced by means of the dumb show in order to enliven a static, declamatory type of tragedy in which events were not represented onstage but were reported at length. In *Locrine* the need for action is no longer pressing because the play itself includes battles and the antics of a clown. Instead, the dumb shows exist primarily to present, in a simplified and striking manner, the moral significance of the play.[29]

The dumb shows preceding Acts I and III illustrate, by means of beast fables, the universal tragic ideas of death and the reversal of fortune. The first dumb show, the visual representation of Death stalking the lion, king of beasts, appropriately introduces a tragedy which begins with the death of Britain's first king and continues with the deaths of most of the principal characters. The third dumb show, a crocodile destroyed by a small snake, presents the moral that pride will have a fall and, presumably, it is meant to apply to the ambitious invader, Humber, who is defeated in the third act but does not drown until the fourth. The remaining three dumb shows use classical stories to comment on Locrine's unhappy love affair. We are introduced to Guendoline's jealousy and her relentless pursuit of Locrine, his mistress and their child, Sabren, in the fifth act, through the fifth dumb show, which exhibits Medea's jealous rage and her disruption of Jason's wedding to the daughter of Creon. The story of Jason and Medea typifies jealousy in the same way that the fourth dumb show, Hercules spinning for Omphale, is illustrative of the notion that a warrior can become a slave to love. In the fourth act, Locrine, after defeating the barbarian invaders, falls in love with Estrild and abandons the responsibilities of his marriage and the kingship. The second dumb show--Perseus' loss of his bride Andromeda on their wedding day--is the least clear in its immediate application to the meaning of the play. The Ovidian story, in which Perseus uses the Gorgon's head to save

[28]*The Elizabethan Dumb Show* (London: Methuen, 1965), p. 61.
[29]*Ibid.*, p. 75. Thelma Greenfield stresses the importance of the dumb show in relation to the themes of the play (*The Induction in Elizabethan Drama* (Eugene: University of Oregon Books, 1969), p. 151): "The early dumb-show inductions related the individual action of the play proper to a universal and abstract plane of axiomatic truths by means of symbolic and stylized representations."

his bride, has been altered to suit the general theme of tragic love and Locrine's loss of Estrild. This romantic interest does not arise, however, until the fourth act; the second act is concerned with Albanact's defeat in battle.

All of the dumb shows in *Locrine* are in the emblem tradition: each presents graphically an action with an abstract and moral meaning, accompanied by a Latin motto.[30] Two of the mottoes seem to have been borrowed from Whitney's *A Choice of Emblemes*[31] and, in any case, there is little doubt that the dramatist intended to transfer the emblematic art onto the stage. The dumb shows simply use actors to present the lesson; the woodcut has become three dimensional. The commentary by Ate is similar to the moral verses underneath the pictures in an emblem book. The two beast fables of the lion and the crocodile have been borrowed directly from Spenser's emblematic poem "Visions of the worlds vanitie"; instead of woodcuts the poem consists of a series of pictorial descriptions each interpreted to show the mutability of greatness.[32]

The dumb shows reveal the influence of several art forms: the classical drama has contributed their choric appearance before each act; the format of illustration followed by a moral explanation is in the emblematic tradition; and the techniques of presentation are closely allied to civic entertainments, such as pageants, Royal Entries and Lord Mayor's Shows.[33] The spectacular entry before each dumb show of Ate, dressed all in black, amid thunder and lightning, with a torch in one hand and a bloody sword in the other, shows an affinity with the pageants. She would instantly gain the audience's attention, and her appearance with the symbols of tragedy would leave no doubt as to the kind of entertainment that was to follow. Ate's function as the presenter and commentator comes from the pageants, but her character does not come from popular entertainment.[34] She is a classical goddess of mischief, described by both Peele (*Tale of Troy*, 11.81-84) and Spenser (*Faerie Queene*, II, vii,55) as the one who threw the golden apple among Venus, Minerva and Athena, their dissension resulting ultimately in the Trojan war. In the play Ate is not the instigator of the tragic action, but rather the one who draws the

---

[30]For further discussion of the relationship between the dumb shows and the emblem tradition, see Rosemary Freeman, *English Emblem Books* (London: Chatto & Windus, 1948), p. 15; Greenfield, *Induction*, p. 21; and Mehl, *Elizabethan Dumb Show*, pp. 13-15, 75.

[31]See n. I,i,1 and n. IV,i,2.

[32]For a discussion of the emblematic nature of this poem and Spenser's imagery in general, see Freeman, *English Emblem Books*, pp. 101-113.

[33]Dieter Mehl focuses on the similarities between the dumb shows and the pageants in *Elizabethan Dumb Show*, pp. 8-9.

[34]See Mehl pp. 72-73 for a description of Ate's role and character.

moral; it seems somewhat inappropriate that the goddess of mischief should speak the epilogue in which she warns that "a woman was the only cause" of the "civil discord." The dumb shows themselves are like simple pageants with formalized action involving a simple reversal of fortune or a symbolic gesture, for example, Omphale striking Hercules with her slipper; conflicting forces are shown by serial entrances or by separate appearances from opposite sides of the stage.[35] The dumb shows in *Gorboduc* are accompanied by music and, possibly, the same was the case in *Locrine*, after the noise of the thunder died down. Symbolic properties are called for--the spinning wheel, showing Hercules' subjection to love, and the wedding garland that bursts into flames while on the head of Creon's daughter. Wild animals are required--a lion, a bear and a crocodile that must fall into a river. In the manner of the civic pageants, the properties, sound effects and balanced groupings of figures combined to impress the meaning of the dumb show upon the audience.

The tragic plot of *Locrine* is constructed around three major battles--two against a foreign invader and one involving a civil war. These battles are linked through a chain of cause and effect based on revenge: Albanact's defeat and death by means of the unheroic tactics of the barbarians are revenged by Locrine; and Locrine's subsequent defeat of Humber leads to the capture of Humber's mistress, Estrild, with whom Locrine falls in love, thus preparing for the second motive of revenge by his wife, Guendoline. This construction of the plot on the basis of revenge is undoubtedly an attempt to imitate the popular success of *The Spanish Tragedy*.[36] An integration of the plot through revenge allowed the author of *Locrine* to capitalize on the popularity of such a revenge device as the ghost, a legacy of Senecan tragedy. The ghost was generally found outside the main action of a play, in the prologue or before and after each act, but in *Locrine* that place is taken by Ate, and two ghosts appear in the midst of the action, those of Albanact and Corineus, both to lend an atmosphere of foreboding and to predict the outcome of battles.

The fact that the battles are shown onstage is significant in the development of a popular drama. In an academic tragedy these battles would have been merely reported; the terrible effects of civil war in *Gorboduc* (V), for example, are described at length while the

---

[35]Greenfield discusses the staging of the dumb shows in *Induction*, pp. 121-141.

[36]Bowers notes (*Elizabethan Revenge Tragedy 1587-1642* (Princeton: Princeton University Press, 1940), pp. 103-104) that the result is not as effective as Kyd's play because "one revenge does not directly determine the other," and, also, because the acts of revenge are not carried out by individuals but by armies.

actual fighting is relegated to dumb show. Long declamatory speeches are still much in evidence in *Locrine*, but they have been adapted to suit the popular demand for episodes of war in plays based on chronicle history. Both before and after the furious activity of battle,[37] the play provides long set speeches appropriate to the occasion; incitements to battle and confrontations, with the exchange of threats and taunts, precede the fighting, and the aftermath includes speeches of triumph or lament.[38] Eleven laments occur in *Locrine*, and five of these come just before a major character commits suicide in despair over the outcome of one of the battles. A long speech at the point of death allowed for the expression of many moral and noble sentiments; the art of dying well is the product of both the native and Senecan literary traditions.[39]

A marked contrast is apparent in the dramatic rhythm of the tragic plot between the short but intense activity of battle and the long set speeches.[40] Most of the action is shown onstage; in only two cases are events of significance reported: the death of Corineus and Locrine's secret visits to Estrild over a period of seven years. Despite the actual representation of major events, a large proportion of stage time is occupied with the set speech. During the delivery of one of these speeches, there was apparently little stage business, apart from stylized movements of the speaker: presumably, the other

---

[37]Chambers describes the usual pattern of the fighting in plays of this type (*The Elizabethan Stage* (Oxford: Clarendon Press, 1923), III, 53): the main part of the battle is not shown, but there are many alarums and excursions where the chief characters confront one another on the outskirts of the conflict; afterwards the defeated flee from battle, and the victors march in triumph.

[38]For a thorough discussion see Clemen, "The Basic Types of Dramatic Set Speech," *English Tragedy*, pp. 44-55.

[39]Theodore Spencer (*Death and Elizabethan Tragedy* (Cambridge: Harvard University Press, 1936), p. 201) points out that the saints' legends established a pattern for a noble death--"the individual made a final speech, commended his soul to the hands of his God, and was carried by angels to heaven." Eliot in his Introduction to *Seneca* (pp. xiv-xv) says that "The posture which gives the greatest opportunity for effect, hence for the Senecan morality, is the posture of dying: death gives his characters the opportunity for their most sententious aphorisms--a hint which Elizabethan dramatists were only too ready to follow."

[40]My discussion of dramatic rhythm is based on the outline given by Wolfgang Clemen in his paper "Shakespeare and Marlowe," presented to the World Shakespeare Congress (*Shakespeare 1971*, ed. Clifford Leech and J.M.R. Margeson (Toronto: University of Toronto Press, 1972), pp. 125-26).

INTRODUCTION   15

characters stood still in a formalized grouping.[41] The
laments in *Locrine* arise from a specific situation, but
such a great deal of time is spent exploring ideas of a
general nature, the fickleness of fortune for example,
that these long speeches become independent of individual
characters.[42] The nature of the dramatic lament, with
its prescribed topics and patterned speech, does not lend
itself to the illumination of character.

Language in the long set speeches in *Locrine* is
characterized by a great amount of repetition, parallelism and the accumulation of mythological example.
Repetition with only minor modulation may occur in a
single line, for example, "These arms, my lord, these
never daunted arms" (I,ii,12), or may extend to several
lines,

> If Fortune favour me in mine attempts,
> Thou shalt be queen of lovely Albion.
> Fortune shall favour me in mine attempts,
> And make thee queen of lovely Albion.   (II,ii,102-5)

The same word may begin several lines in succession (I,ii,
52-55) or conclude several lines in succession (IV,iii,
15-20). In a few cases the last word of one line becomes
the subject of the next, for example in Estrild's
description of Britain,

> The airy hills enclosed with shady groves,
> The groves replenished with sweet chirping birds,
> The birds resounding heavenly melody. (II,ii,36-38)

F.G. Hubbard in his study of the repetition and parallelism in Elizabethan drama claims that the closer a play is
to Seneca the more examples of repetition and parallelism
it contains;[43] *Locrine* is a good illustration: "No
other play of the earlier Elizabethan drama contains so
many examples, such elaborate ones, and so great a
variety of forms."[44] The long speeches are not construct-

---

[41]Muriel C. Bradbrook, *Elizabethan Stage Conditions* (Hamden, Conn.: Archon Books, 1962), pp. 109-10; for additional discussion of formal acting, see Alfred Harbage, "Elizabethan Acting," *PMLA*, 54 (1939), 685-708, and Marvin Rosenberg, "Elizabethan Actors: Men or Marionettes?" *PMLA*, 69 (1954), 915-927.

[42]See Clemen, "The Set Speech in Renaissance Drama," *English Tragedy*, pp. 37-38.

[43]"Repetition and Parallelism in the Earlier Elizabethan Drama," *PMLA*, 20 (1905), 369.

[44]*Ibid.*, p. 374.

ed by means of a logical progression in the argument, but rather through the addition of detail, especially mythological examples, in parallel structures.[45] Imagery of the underworld, including its geography and inhabitants, is repeated throughout the play. In true Senecan fashion, a reference to one of the damned inevitably triggers a list of two or three of his companions;[46] Humber, for example, refers to three victims of Jove's justice in two lines, "Tantal's hunger or Ixion's wheel,/ Or to the vulture of Prometheus" (III,vii,46-47). Estrild's speech in which she describes the pastoral beauty of the island (II,ii,33-50) is the most notable exception to the usual description of war and the underworld.

A common pattern for each scene in the tragic plot is the entrance of the protagonist and retinue, the exchange of long speeches and a general exit. Seldom does another character enter *in medias res*: the two noteworthy exceptions are the entrances of Strumbo, the clown, and Estrild, both of whom may have been later additions to the play. The comic subplot, on the other hand, introduces great activity onstage, frequent entries and exits and an interaction between characters by means of quick exchanges in the dialogue. In the tragic plot, few simple utterances occur and the transition from set speech to dialogue is awkward, when a character becomes aware of the others on the stage and directs his remarks to them only in the last few lines of a long monologue.[47] The modern reader would probably find the comedy more realistic in action and speech than the bombastic, stilted tragic plot; the doubtful inference follows that a greater naturalism is a progression in dramatic technique and, therefore, that the comic subplot may be seen as superior. The intention of the dramatist in the tragic plot, however, was to impose a pattern on experience through the repetition of set topics and rhetorical devices; in this kind of tragedy, the greater the emotion and complexity of thought, the greater was the artificiality of language.[48]

In each of the first four acts of *Locrine* there is a comic intrusion, and the comic episodes are unified

---

[45]Wolfgang Clemen provides a valuable discussion of the language in *Locrine* in his chapter on the play in *English Tragedy Before Shakespeare*; see especially pp. 95-97.

[46]Frank Laurence Lucas, *Seneca and Elizabethan Tragedy* (Cambridge: Cambridge University Press, 1922), p. 65; John William Cunliffe, *Influence of Seneca on Elizabethan Tragedy* (London: Macmillan, 1893), p. 45.

[47]See Clemen, *English Tragedy*, p. 93, n. 1.

[48]R.F. Hill, "Shakespeare's Early Tragic Mode," *Shakespeare Quarterly*, 9 (1958), 462: "...in the early tragedies and histories all occurrences of markedly stylized dialogue and word-play will be found to be related to the disturbed feelings of the speakers. The more intense the feelings, the more artificial the language."

through the person of Strumbo, who assumes a number of different roles, including that of a courtier, rustic, comic lover and comic soldier. In drama of a similar type, *Cambises* or *Horestes*, for example, it was common for the presence of the clown to be the single unifying factor in a series of comic episodes. Often these scenes would have no relevance to the themes of the serious plot, and their sole purpose was one of diversion. The attempt has been made in *Locrine*, however, to integrate the comic subplot with the tragedy; in his roles as lover and soldier, Strumbo provides a humorous comment on the serious concerns of the main plot, and the comic scenes parody bombastic language, the prevailing style of the tragedy. In four of the comic episodes, Strumbo comes into direct contact with the tragic characters. Two other episodes, Strumbo's wooing of Dorothy and his forced submission to Margery, are apparently independent of the main plot, but they do, in fact, undercut the romantic conventions surrounding Locrine's love for Estrild by making the symptoms of love look ridiculous and by placing romance beside realistic desire.[49]

As a rule in a tragedy with a comic subplot, the action is directed from the tragedy to the comedy;[50] events in the tragic plot profoundly affect the comic characters, especially when the tragedy concerns a king at war, as in *The Famous Victories* or *Locrine*, and then the comic characters represent the common people.[51] Strumbo's contented life as a cobbler is rudely interrupted when he is pressed into Albanact's army (II,iii). An analogous scene occurs in *The Famous Victories* (ll. 1208-50) when Dericke and John Cobler are forced to accept press-money. Strumbo's life is shown to be further affected by war when he reports directly to the king that the enemy has burnt his home, including his wife (II,iv); a concern for the protection of his people is Albanact's primary motive of revenge against the Scythian invaders. The comic soldier was a familiar role for the Elizabethan clown, and traditionally the soldier-clown was a coward. In *The Famous Victories*, Dericke's favourite tactic was to feign injury in order to be excused from the fighting, and he proudly claims after the battle that he was "foure or fiue times slaine" (l.1850). Strumbo feigns death on the battlefield, a Falstaffian trick, and Trompart, his man, laments his death in doggerel. Trompart uses the traditional topics

---

[49]As Brian Vickers points out (*The Artistry of Shakespeare's Prose* (London: Methuen, 1968), pp. 16, 24, 43), Shakespeare's clowns characteristically deflate the idealistic pretensions of the characters in the main plot through imagery and exaggerated "rhetorical symmetry."

[50]Richard Levin, *The Multiple Plot in English Renaissance Drama* (Chicago: University of Chicago Press, 1971), p. 221.

[51]William Empson, *Some Versions of Pastoral* (London: Chatto & Windus, 1935), p. 29.

--rhetorical question, apostrophe, calling on nature and on other people to assist in the mourning[52]--but the homely content, organized into rhyming fourteeners, is inappropriate to the formal lament. This comic eulogy follows immediately after Albanact's long lament against fortune, concluded by six lines of Latin in which he appeals to the infernal deities to receive his body. The existence of a parody beside the serious lament is perhaps an indication that the comedy is a later addition to a tragedy written in a style that was rapidly becoming old-fashioned and subject to ridicule.

When Strumbo plays the role of an eloquent lover (I,iii), he reduces the conventions of ideal romance to the literal and vulgar. Strumbo characteristically deflates his elaborate conceits and flowery phrases with a homely image. He begins with an astrological explanation for his misfortunes as a lover, referring to the elements, planets, stars, moon and even the philosopher Lactantius; the conceit comes to an abrupt halt when he concludes that all "goeth arseward" (I,iii,6). Strumbo parodies the suffering lover by comparing his own tears, "from the wat'ry fountains of my most dainty fair eyes" (I,iii,8-9), to the water running from bucking-tubs. Using the same parallelism and balance found in the language of the main plot, Strumbo makes fun of the lover, like Locrine, who suffers because he has seen and heard the fair lady:

Ah, Strumbo,
what hast thou seen?   not Dina with the Ass Tom?
Yea, with these eyes thou hast seen her,
and therefore pull them out for they will work thy bale.

Ah, Strumbo,
what hast thou heard?   not the voice of the nightingale,
but a voice sweeter than hers;
yea, with these ears hast thou heard it,
and therefore cut them off, for they have caused thy sorrow.
(I,iii,17-24)

Strumbo pursues this argument to its absurd limits by saying that he must kill himself, but mundane reality undercuts this romantic convention of dying for love when he realizes that he would have to leave his mistress. Strumbo aptly describes his affectation in language as "grand verbosity" (I,iii,29). He makes learned allusions, generally mispronounced, to Lactantius and his book of "Constultations" (I,iii,5), to Dina and Cuprit, and he intersperses his speech with perverted Italian phrases, such as "*succado de labres*" (I,iii,98).[53] Strumbo's

[52]Wolfgang Clemen describes Trompart's parody of the traditional lament in *English Tragedy*, pp. 261-262.

[53]Olive Mary Busby (*Studies in the Development of the Fool in the Elizabethan Drama* (London: Oxford University Press, 1923), pp. 55, 78) notes that this language is typical of the "grandiloquent style"

INTRODUCTION   19

manner of speech is generally roundabout with so many
flowery phrases and conceits that he is in danger of
being misunderstood. Although Strumbo makes his first
appearance in the third scene of the play and Locrine
does not declare his love for Estrild until the fourth
act, the clown's deflation of romantic convention and his
parody of bombastic language may be said to apply directly to the main plot.

When Strumbo appears as the rustic lover (III,iv), he
speaks in the vernacular, using a natural rhythm and
proverbial expressions.[54] His comic companion, Oliver,
speaks with a stage brogue, a common source of humour,
apparent in such characters as Hodge in *Horestes*, Hob and
Lob in *Cambises* and Grim the Collier in *Damon and Pythias*.
When Strumbo is a courtly lover, his humour is derived
from mocking the affectation in language, but when he is
a rustic lover, his slapstick comedy is based on name-
calling and fighting. Strumbo is forced by Margery's
father and brother to pay for his sexual license and to
agree to marry Margery. A parallel may be drawn with the
main plot when father and son, Corineus and Thrasimachus,
force Locrine to honour his marriage contract to Guendoline. Margery is the one, in fact, who beats Strumbo
into submission; a similar episode occurs in *The Famous
Victories* (x) when John Cobler's wife beats Dericke.
Strumbo is schooled by blows, and he is the victim of the
abusive rhetoric of the "University of Bridewell" (III,
iv,33).[55]

The last of the comic scenes in *Locrine* (IV,iii)
begins with a monologue by Strumbo on the tribulations of
his married life with Margery. This domestic picture
follows immediately after Locrine's declaration of his
love for Estrild; the idealized love affair is undercut
by the conflict and realistic desire in Strumbo's
marriage. A typical source of humour for the Elizabethan
clown is the jibe against women and marriage. The meeting between Strumbo and Humber in this scene, when the
clown is mistaken for Mercury, again brings the subplot
into contact with the main plot.

of Elizabethan clowns. K.M. Lea, in *Italian Popular Comedy* (Oxford:
The Clarendon Press, 1934), II, 399-400, suggests that the Zanni,
clowns of the Commedia Dell' Arte, may have had some influence on the
behaviour of the lover, Strumbo, particularly on his habit of per-
verting words.

[54]Busby describes this type of clown speech as the "vigorous
vernacular" (*Development of the Fool*, p. 78).

[55]C.R. Baskervill in his book *The Elizabethan Jig and Related Song
Drama* (Chicago: University of Chicago Press, 1929), pp. 331-332
compares this comic scene with one in a German comedy, *Tiberius and
Anabella* (acted by English comedians by 1604), where the clown, Hans,
is forced into marriage by a father and daughter (I,ii). Both plays
are similar to a German jig called "Harlequins Hochzeit"; the jig
also contains "abusive epithets" and fighting.

Strumbo acts as the comic counterpart of Ate when he draws a moral from his love affairs. He instructs the lovers in the audience how to bring their affairs to a happy conclusion: "If any of you be in love, provide ye a capcase full of new coined words, and then shall you soon have the *succado de labres*, and something else" (I,iii,96-99). The irony of his advice is that his learned vocabulary led only to confusion until he expressed his love in simple language. After his defeat at the hands of Margery and his submission to marriage, Strumbo comments ruefully, "O Codpiece, thou hast done thy master; this it is to be meddling with warm plackets" (III,iv,57-58). Strumbo's habit of addressing the audience directly, whether it be to ask for a knife to sharpen his pen or to inquire after the audience's health, "How do you, masters, how do you? how have you 'scaped hanging this long time?" (IV,iii,21-22), is in the tradition of clowns such as Ambidexter who exist both as characters in the dramas and as independent commentators, licensed to make satirical remarks.

The structure of *Locrine* reveals a combination of two traditions: the appearance of dumb shows before each act, which in their choric function are derived ultimately from classical drama, and the large amount of stage time devoted to long rhetorical speeches in the style of Seneca are characteristic of academic drama; and the inclusion of the antics of a clown shows the influence of popular drama. While the evidence is not overwhelming, the fact that revision has taken place in the play in order to include at least one comic episode, the meeting between Strumbo and Humber, suggests that perhaps *Locrine* is an academic play that has been revised with a view to the popular taste.

4. HISTORICAL THEMES

Locrine may be defined as a history play because it is based on chronicle history, generally accepted in Elizabethan times as true, and this account of Britain's Trojan ancestors presents a useful lesson on the art of ruling.[56] The political morality provides both a positive and negative example; an English king defeating foreign invaders would appeal to a sense of nationalism, while, on the negative side, the plot involves a division of the kingdom and the presence of an immoral ruler.

Early in the sixteenth century the historical validity of the *Historia Regum Britanniae*, the foundation of early British history, was questioned by Polydore Vergil, an Italian commissioned by Henry VIII to write a definitive history of Britain. Polydore Vergil states in his *Historia Anglica* (pp. 18-19), "*Equidem nihil occultius,*

---

[56] For a discussion of the purposes of the history play, see Irving Ribner, *The English History Play in the Age of Shakespeare* (Princeton: Princeton University Press, 1957), pp. 12-27.

nihil incertius, nihil ignoratius rebus Britannorũ à principio gestis." The English historians, however, adopt a tolerant attitude toward Geoffrey's account of their noble origins; every nation desires an heroic beginning, and early history must necessarily contain fabulous elements because the great distance in time makes any proof difficult if not impossible. The will to believe in the Trojan myth is evident by its inclusion in the English chronicles, generally preceded by a note of justification in the preface. At the beginning of his *Annales* (pp. 6-7), John Stow includes "A briefe Proofe of Brvte"; he says that he will follow the "common opinion" according to Geoffrey of Monmouth, and, although he cannot "precisely defend, that he [Brutus] was descended of *Aeneas* or *Silvius*, or came hither by Oracle accompanied with *Troians*," he can affirm that "there was one *Brute*, or *Brito*, King of this Realme, which left it to his posterity" (p. 6).[57] In his *Britannia*, William Camden, while not trying to impose his views on any man, says that he, too, will support the "receiv'd opinion" (p. vi) and allow the history of Brutus. Camden acknowledges that every nation desires a noble ancestry:

> For my part, it shall never trouble me, if *Brutus* pass current for the father and founder of the *British* Nation. Let the *Britains* descent stand good, as they deduce it from the Trojans. I shall never contradict it: nay, I shall shew you hereafter, how with truth it may be maintained. I am not ignorant, that in old time Nations had recourse to *Hercules*, in later ages to the *Trojans*, for their originals. And let antiquity herein be pardoned, if she sometimes disguise the truth with the mixture of a fable, and bring in the Gods themselves to act a part, when she design'd thereby to render the beginnings, either of a city, or of a nation, more noble and majestical. (p. ix)

In the prologue to *The Cronycles of Englande and of dyvorc other realmes*, Rastell says that he will not deny the Trojan legend but, on the other hand, he cannot "precisely affirme it." Apart from any historical authenticity, Rastell justifies Geoffrey of Monmouth's account as a moral exemplum on kingship:

---

[57]Stow attacks Polydore Vergil for attempting to deny the noble ancestry of the British people:
...*Polidore* an Italian, though learned, yet with a vaineglorious enuy, to aduance his owne Country, will not endure that any other Countrey shall have monuments of antiquity. And whereas the rest onely except against *Brute*, this man with one dash of a pen, cashireth threescore Princes together, with all their histories and Historians, yea, and some ancient Lawes also:...(p. 7).

...a man may se many notable examples of divers noble princes ȳ wisely & virtuesly governed theire people which may be an example to prĭcis now liuing to use the same...and also how diuers princis and grete mĕ exaltid in pride and ambicion using tiranny & cruelte or ells being neclygĕt in governyng of theyre people or giffing them self to vicious liffing were euer by the stroke of god ponished for the same....

In the seventeenth century, Milton in his *History of Britain* (pp. 2-3) says that "nothing certain" is known about the period of history from the time of the first inhabitants to the arrival of Julius Caesar, and although many have rejected the account given by Geoffrey of Monmouth as fable, the fact remains that many learned men have accepted the Trojan myth as the "approved story."[58] The English historical writers do not press the question of the factual accuracy of the *Historia Regum Britanniae*; instead, they value Geoffrey's chronicle on moral and patriotic grounds, as an example of kingship and as a link with the heroes of the past.

One purpose of fundamental importance to the history play is to enhance the patriotic feelings of the audience, and a common way of doing this is through the representation of an English king victorious over a foreign army.[59] Locrine defeats the barbaric usurper, Humber, but only after the Huns have invaded Britain, weakened through division, and taken control of Scotland by defeating Albanact's army. The English defeat, however, is not the result of weakness; the barbarians use a military stratagem or policy, whereby Albanact's men are ambushed from behind. The dramatist is so intent on glorifying the English that, in the midst of battle, Humber pauses to extol Albanact's courage. Humber and his men are often described as Scythians, and Humber vaunts in the idiom of Tamburlaine, thus allying himself with the Marlovian hero, an immoral usurper. After Humber's death, the ghost of Albanact provides the political moral:

> Lo, here the gift of fell ambition,
> Of usurpation and of treachery.
> Lo, here the harms that wait upon all those
> That do intrude themselves in others' lands
> Which are not under their dominion. (IV,iii,89-93)

The whole subject of *Locrine*, the noble beginnings of the British nation, has a patriotic appeal; the play, in addition, shows the derivations of place names from

---

[58] Milton will include the material contained in the *Historia* if for no other reason "...but in favour of our English Poets, and Rhetoricians, who by thir Art will know, how to use them judiciously" (p. 3).

[59] David Riggs discusses the patriotic appeal of the history play in *Shakespeare's Heroical Histories* (Cambridge: Harvard University Press, 1971), p. 60.

the names of popular heroes and heroines. The dramatization of the legends surrounding the naming of the Humber and Severn rivers, the traditional boundaries of the three kingdoms of Britain, comprises a major part of the action. The river goddess Sabrina, after whom the Severn is named, appears in the river mythologies of Spenser, Drayton, and Milton. As Tatlock points out in his study of the *Historia Regum Britanniae*, the eponymous names of Locrine, Albanact and Camber were probably all invented by Geoffrey of Monmouth in order to establish a firm foundation for the beginning of the *Historia*.[60] Cornwall is derived from the name of Corineus. Both Corineus and his adversary, the giant Gogmagog, are popular figures in the civic pageants,[61] and part of the entertainment provided for Elizabeth's procession through London before her coronation was at "...Temple Barre, which was dressed fynelye with the two ymages of Gotmagot the Albione, and Corineus the Briton, two gyantes bigge in stature...".[62] The name of the capital city, Troynovant or new Troy, establishes a sense of continuity with the herioc past.[63]

The Trojan myth not only links British history with the distant past but also with the future through the prophecy of Merlin. In the *Historia* (VII,3), Merlin predicts that Cadwallader, a king in the line of Brutus, will drive the Saxons out and reunite the country. In his discussion of the Trojan legend, Parsons stresses the political importance of descent from Brutus by citing the example of Henry VII who supported his claim to the throne by emphasizing his Welsh descent through Cadwallader. He even named his son Arthur, thus proclaiming to the people that at last a second Arthur had come to bring peace and stability to Britain.[64] In Peele's *Edward I*, Lluellen also supports his claim to the throne through his descent from Cadwallader:

> Follow Lluellen rightfull prince of Wales,
> Sprong from the loines of great Cadwallader,
> Discended from the loines of Trojan Brute. (ii,270-72)

[60]*The Legendary History of Britain* (Berkeley: University of California Press, 1950), pp. 149, 395.

[61]Alice Sylvia Venezky, *Pageantry on the Shakespearian Stage* (New York: Twayne Publishers, 1951), p. 175: "In the history of the pageant, perhaps the most popular single figure was the giant, beloved member of the earliest folk festivals and civic celebrations in England and on the continent."

[62]John Nichols, *The Progresses and Public Processions of Queen Elizabeth* (London: John Nichols and Son, 1823), I, 55.

[63]The arrival of Brutus is pinpointed exactly in relation to the history of the world by Holinshed, who claims that Brutus changed the name of the island from Albion to Britain "...in the 1116. before Christ, and 2850. after the creation of the world" (p. 4).

[64]"The Trojan Legend in England," *Modern Language Review*, 24 (1929), 398.

In *The Faerie Queene*, Spenser pays an elaborate compliment to Elizabeth by tracing her ancestry from the arrival of Brutus. Merlin prophesies in the poem that one descendant of Britomart and Artegall, namely Elizabeth, will eventually restore British rule and unify the country: "Thenceforth eternall vnion shall be made/...Then shall a royall virgin raine" (III,iii,49).

Allusions to the Trojan legend would remind the contemporary audience both of their noble ancestry and of the country's original unity and its subsequent loss with Brutus' decision to divide his kingdom. The longing to restore this unity is the subject of a pageant, "The Triumphs of Re-United Britania," written by Anthony Munday in honour of the entrance of the new Lord Mayor, Sir Leonard Holliday, October 29, 1605.[65] In the description of the show, James I is represented as the second Brutus:

> ...by whose happye comming to the Crowne, England, Wales, and Scotland, by the first Brute severed and divided, are in our second Brute re-united and made one happy Britania again. Peace and quietness brining that to passe, which warre nor any other meanes could attaine unto. For ioy of which sacred Union and combination, Locrine, Camber, and Albanact, figured there also in their antique estates, deliver up theyr Crownes and Sceptres, applauding the day of this long-wisht conjunction, and Troya-nova (now London) incites fair Thamesis, and the rivers that bounded the severed Kingdoms (personated in faire and beautifull Nymphs) to sing Paeans and Songs of Triumph, in honor of our second Brute, Royall King James.[66]

One of the principal lessons in kingship that emerge from the succession of rulers in the *Historia Regum Britanniae* is the danger inherent in a division of the kingdom. Near the end of his chronicle, Geoffrey states that it is "against the ancient traditions of the island that the single sovereignty of the crown should be divided..." (XII,3). Throughout the *Historia*, the kingdom is divided many times; in the line of Brutus, three of the most significant divisions are carried out by Brutus himself, by Lear, the tenth king, and, finally, by Gorboduc, the eighteenth king. In each of the dramatizations of these reigns, *Locrine*, the two versions of the Lear story--*King Leir* and Shakespeare's *Lear*--and *Gorboduc*, the initial action concerns an aged king dividing his land equally among his children. One of the consequences of this division is the threat of foreign invasion and, in both *Locrine* and *King Leir*, such a foreign invasion is successful. The ghost of Albanact in

---

[65]*Ibid.*, p. 403.
[66]John Nichols, *Progresses, Processions, and Magnificent Festivities of King James The First* (London: J.B. Nichols, 1828), I, 569.

The Mirror For Magistrates draws an explicit moral from Brutus' division of his kingdom:

> ...now it was deuided all
> Into three parts, and might within a while
> Be won, by force, by treason, fraude or guile. (11.556-58)

    Brutus divides the kingdom when he is about to die, and thus he is not guilty of trying to free himself from the cares of ruling. Lear and Gorboduc wish to evade both the problem of primogeniture, whereby the oldest child is the sole successor, and the responsibilities of the kingship. As Irving Ribner suggests in his discussion of *King Lear*, these responsibilities were ordained by God; the abdication of the king was thus a violation of the natural order, and the universal chaos stemming from Lear's abandonment of the kingship and his division of the kingdom is apparent throughout the play on each level of existence.[67] The division of power creates rival factions of equal strength within the royal family; when these factions come into conflict the result is civil war, and, in both *Gorboduc* and *King Lear*, the royal family is annihilated, leaving the country without an heir to the throne. In the *Historia*, Geoffrey speaks out strongly against civil war by citing the Gospel: "...'Every kingdom divided against itself shall be made desolate and the house shall fall upon the house!'" (XI, 9). One of Gorboduc's counsellors tries to dissuade him from his intention to divide the kingdom by citing the mistake of Brutus:

> The mighty Brute, first prince of all this land,
> Possessed the same, and ruled it well in one:
> He, thinking that the compass did suffice
> For his three sons three kingdoms eke to make,
> Cut it in three, as you would now in twain.
> But how much British blood hath since been spilt,
> To join again the sunder'd unity! (I,ii,270-76)

    In the second chapter of *The Governor*, Elyot describes the best form of government as that which has only one ruler: "...undoubtedly the best and most sure governance is by one king or prince" (p. 7). He uses an example from the British chronicles: when the Saxons drove the Britons out of the country and the "realm was divided into sundry regions or kingdoms" (p. 11), Britain was almost reduced to ruins through constant warfare until King Edgar restored the single monarchy. The reign of Brutus, while bringing to mind the glorious past, also contained a political warning about the consequences involved in a division of the kingdom.

---

[67]*Patterns in Shakespearian Tragedy* (London: Methuen, 1960), p. 118.

The reign of Locrine is illustrative of the disastrous consequences of the immoral ruler, a theme common to many history plays. Plays such as *A Knack To Know A Knave*, *James IV*, *The Misfortunes of Arthur*, *King John and Matilda* and *Edward III* all have a major concern with royal adultery and the necessity of the ruler's self-control as a prerequisite to good government. The virtuous life of the ruler is reflected in his kingdom and, similarly, the effects of a bad king are seen in the immorality of his subjects, the disaffection and desertion of the nobles, civil war, and foreign invasion.

In *A Knack To Know A Knave*, a play using legendary history as a moral exemplum, King Edgar heeds the advice of his good counsellor, Dunstan, and gains control over his illicit passions by calling to mind the fate of adulterers, in particular Locrine:

> For he deserues not other to command,
> That hath no power to maister his desire,
> For Locrin being the eldest sonne of Brute,
> Did dote so far upon an Almaine maid,
> And was so rauisht with her pleasing sight,
> That full seuen yeares he kept her under earth,
> Euen in the lyfe time of faire Guendolin:
> Which made the Cornish men to rise in Armes,
> And neuer left till Locrin was slaine:
> And now though late, at last I call to minde,
> What wretched ends fell to Adulterers. (ll.1731-41)

Both Locrine and Mordred, in *The Misfortunes of Arthur*, persist in carrying out the dictates of their own passions, and they are both destroyed by civil war, the worst evil that could befall a kingdom. Both are convinced that the king's will is law: Locrine refuses to be dissuaded from his love for Estrild in his belief that "Kings need not fear the vulgar sentences" (IV,ii,138); similarly, Mordred assumes "The Lawes doe licence as the Soueraigne lists" (II,ii,25). James IV, "misled by lust" (Induction, 1.107), violates the sacrament of marriage and betrays the trust of his nobles; in order to satisfy his desire, he will risk all, even the destruction of his kingdom:

> And for fair Ida will I hazard life,
> Venture my kingdom, country, and my crown:
> Such fire hath love to burn a kingdom down. (I,i,170-172)

The Scottish nobles form an alliance with the English king, and an invasion is prevented only through James' sudden reformation. The nobles in *King John and Matilda*, disenchanted with the king's wilful rule and his adulterous pursuit of Fitzwater's daughter, join forces with the Dauphin, but the threat of the French army actually assisted by the English nobility is enough to bring about King John's moral improvement.

Edward III is more successful than *Locrine* in dealing with the same political themes: a victorious English army and the king's adultery. In *Edward III*, however, the sequence of action is reversed: Edward overcomes his illicit passion for the Countess of Salisbury; then he tests his nobility in the just war against the French. Edward, unlike Locrine, is able to conquer his unlawful love, and his self-control is a lesson in kingship, showing that the strength of the kingdom is dependent on the personal virtue of the ruler. Although Locrine is successful in defeating the foreign invaders, he brings about his own downfall by falling in love with the mistress of his enemy. The focus in *Locrine* is on the representation of history rather than on the tragic hero as in *Edward III*; the individual tragedy of Locrine occurs only in the second half of the play, the first part of which is concerned with Brutus' division of his kingdom and Albanact's defeat by foreign invaders. The period of history contained in Locrine is important both as a glorification of the British past and as a political lesson on the dangers of a divided kingdom and an immoral ruler.

5. AUTHORSHIP

The initials "W.S." on the title-page of *Locrine* led to the inclusion of the play in the Third Folio of Shakespeare's plays (1664), and subsequently in the Fourth Folio (1689). The folio editors included seven plays[68] which had not been included in the First Folio of 1623. As a result of previous title-page ascriptions, they believed that these plays had been written by Shakespeare; two, *Thomas Lord Cromwell* (1602) and *The Puritan* (1607), also have ascriptions to "W.S." on their title-pages. The most likely explanation for these ascriptions is that Shakespeare's initials appearing on a play not actually written by him would help stimulate sales by suggesting to a prospective buyer that he was getting the work of a successful playwright. This may have been the case with *Thomas Lord Cromwell* and *The Puritan*, but the date of *Locrine*, 1595, is too early to permit capitalization on Shakespeare's success, at least in the area of printed plays, because it is not until 1598 that Shakespeare is acknowledged as the author of his own plays on the title-pages of *Richard II*, *Richard III*, and *Love's Labour's Lost*. The first quartos of several plays by Shakespeare --*Titus Andronicus* (1594), *The Taming of the Shrew* (1594), *Richard II* (1597), *Richard III* (1597), *Henry IV, Part I* (1598)--were all printed with no indication of authorship. Shakespeare's success in the theatre, on the other hand, may have been sufficient by 1595 to help a publisher sell

---

[68]*The Puritan, Thomas Lord Cromwell, Locrine, Oldcastle, The London Prodigal, A Yorkshire Tragedy* and *Pericles*.

his books by means of a fraudulent ascription to Shakespeare.

The professional reputation of Thomas Creede, the printer of *Locrine*, is important in trying to assess the validity of the ascription to "W.S." His work records a clear association with Shakespeare.[69] He printed four bad quartos of Shakespeare's plays: *The First Part of the Contention of York and Lancaster* (for Thomas Millington, 1594), *Henry V* (for Thomas Millington and John Busby in 1600 and again for Pavier in 1602), *The Merry Wives of Windsor* (for Johnson, 1602). He produced, as well, a reprint of the reported text of *Richard III* (1597) for Andrew Wise in 1598 and 1602 and a good quarto of *Romeo and Juliet* (1599) for Cuthbert Burby. Two plays related to Shakespeare's that Creede printed independently--*The True Tragedy of Richard III* and *The Famous Victories*--are bad quartos. In all of these, no mention is made of Shakespeare's authorship except on the title-pages of the 1598 and 1602 quartos of *Richard III*, which correctly state that the play is "By William Shake-speare." Although Creede produced six bad quartos of Shakespeare's plays or plays closely related to those by Shakespeare, in four cases he was merely acting as the printer for a publisher who secured the copy.

The other source of contemporary evidence concerning Creede's professional integrity, apart from the plays he printed, is his record in the Stationers' Company. Two entries in the Stationers' Register cite fines paid by Creede, one for sixpence for failing to appear on the quarter day (Arber,II,823) and another for two shillings sixpence for neglecting to present an apprentice (Arber, II,823). Judging by the amount paid, the second offence would appear to be more serious but, actually, it was not unusual among the master printers,[70] and Creede continued to have the services of his apprentice.

The possibility remains that Creede was not trying to deceive anyone by using the initials "W.S." on the title-page of *Locrine*. At a time when the majority of plays were printed anonymously, it was not uncommon for the printer to use initials alone to indicate authorship; Creede uses initials, apparently correct, on two other plays which he printed independently, *Menaechmi* and *Alphonsus*.[71] "W.S." may refer to a lesser known poet,

---

[69]Leo Kirschbaum outlines Creede's association with Shakespeare in *Shakespeare and the Stationers* (Columbus: Ohio State University Press, 1955), p. 295.

[70]George Walton Williams, "The Good Quarto of *Romeo and Juliet*, A Bibliographical Study," Ph.D. dissertation, University of Virginia, 1957, pp. 3-4, n.6.; in the opinion of Kirschbaum, *Shakespeare and the Stationers*, p. 296, "Creede's record in the Stationers' Company was apparently without blemish."

[71]See Maxwell, *Shakespeare Apocrypha*, pp. 5-7, for a detailed discussion of the use of initials on the title-pages of plays printed from 1590 to 1610.

playwright or actor whose actual involvement in the writing or refurbishing of *Locrine* may be seen to have been small or great, depending on how the phrases "Newly set forth, overseen and corrected,/ By W.S." are interpreted. The question arises whether the phrase "By W.S." is meant to refer to the whole play or only to the revisions; the more likely case would be that "W.S." is the reviser. Candidates for the initials "W.S.", besides Shakespeare, include William Smith, the author of a collection of sonnets, *Chloris*; or, *The Complaint of the Passionate Despised Shepheard* (1596); William Stanley, Earl of Derby, who supported his own company of actors (1594-1618); and Wentworth Smith, frequently mentioned by Henslowe in the years 1601-1603 as a collaborator in the writing of plays.[72] It is possible but not probable that any of these three men may have had some connection with *Locrine*: William Smith is not known to have written for the stage; William Stanley would probably have produced plays for the Derby's Men, and there is reason to believe that *Locrine* was connected with the Queen's Men;[73] and the dramatic activity of Wentworth Smith is six years later than the date of publication of *Locrine*. Another candidate is William Smyght, one of three players recorded by Henslowe (I,6; II,312) to have witnessed a loan on June 1, 1595 to his nephew, Francis, a member of the Queen's Company. Another actor with the right initials, William Sheppard, is mentioned by Chambers in the *Elizabethan Stage* (II,339). We cannot assume that either Smyght or Sheppard was involved in writing as well as in acting plays.

Locrine has been variously attributed to Shakespeare, Marlowe, Kyd, Peele and Greene. These attributions are based generally on parallel passages and on impressionistic assumptions with respect to metrical tests, imagery, character and theme. The vaunting speeches of ambition in *Tamburlaine* have influenced *Locrine* and so have the revenge structure and the elaborate rhetorical devices of *The Spanish Tragedy*. These plays of Marlowe and Kyd were a great success, and it seems inevitable that a lesser dramatist writing for the popular stage would try to capitalize on their success. When impressionistic tests are used to attribute *Locrine* to Peele, an equally valid case using the same criteria, can be made for Greene. The poetical speeches, for example, often used to ascertain Peele's hand in the play[74] are balanced by the low comedy routines said to be characteristic of Greene.[75] Parallel passages are numerous in *Locrine*, but unfortun-

---

[72]Maxwell explores some of the possible solutions to the mystery of "W.S." in *Shakespeare Apocrypha*, pp. 7-13, 69.

[73]See Introduction, pp. 32-34.

[74]Leonard R. N. Ashley, *Authorship and Evidence* (Genève: Librairie Droz, 1968), p. 70.

[75]Ribner, *English History Play*, pp. 237-238.

ately the weight of parallel passages does not tip the balance in favour of any one dramatist[76] if, indeed, parallel passages by themselves could be used to determine authorship.[77] Not only does *Locrine* borrow from the most popular dramatic works but also from popular non-dramatic works, for example, *The Faerie Queene*, Whitney's *A Choice of Emblemes*, *The Mirror For Magistrates* and Seneca's tragedies. The author of *Locrine* is well acquainted with contemporary literature, and his sensitivity to popular taste is apparent in his creation of a play which has a variety of appeals, for example, spectacle, comedy, romance, and battles.

If we can trust Buc's conjecture about Charles Tilney's authorship of *Locrine*, then the problem of attribution of at least the earliest version of *Locrine* is solved. Most scholars, however, have favoured either Peele or Greene as the author of *Locrine*. Peele was the most popular candidate in the late nineteenth and early twentieth centuries, but now, with the relationship to *Selimus* emphasized, the tendency has been to lean toward Greene as the author or reviser of *Locrine*. The history of attribution of *The Tragical Reign of Selimus* has a direct bearing on the study of *Locrine* because of the close relationship between the two plays. If both plays were written or revised by the same man, then a solution to the problem of attribution for *Selimus* would naturally answer the question of authorship for *Locrine*. *Selimus* became associated with the name of Robert Greene when it was discovered that several passages from *Selimus* were ascribed to Greene in *England's Parnassus*. Although Churton Collins, an editor of Greene's works, refuses to include *Selimus* on the basis of such an unreliable authority as Allot's anthology, Tucker Brooke, the editor of *The Shakespeare Apocrypha*, sees the influence of Greene in *Selimus*. He claims a relationship between *Selimus* and two of Greene's early plays, *Orlando Furioso* and *Alphonsus*, in the mythological reference, the general dramatic structure and the number and kinds of borrowings from Spenser, Marlowe and Greene. In *Locrine*, also, he finds two features of Greene's work, the borrowing of lines and phrases and the copying of the most fashionable plot and dramatic structure. He considers *Locrine* an early play by Greene, written before the playwright fell under the spell of *Tamburlaine*. In the chronology of Greene's plays, Tucker Brooke places *Locrine* first, to be

---

[76]Cf. Hubbard, "*Locrine* and *Selimus*," p. 31: "If, now, we use the evidence of parallel passages in the cases of *Locrine* and *Selimus*, we shall surely arrive at no certain results. These plays have borrowed so much from so many sources, that, on the evidence of parallel passages, they can be ascribed to almost any of the predecessors of Shakespeare."

[77]For guidelines concerning the validity of parallel passages as evidence see M. St. Clare Byrne, "Bibliographical Clues in Collaborate Plays," *Library*, 4th ser., 13(1933), 21-48.

followed by *Selimus, Orlando, Alphonsus*, with a culmination of Greene's style in *James IV*. Irving Ribner considers *Selimus*, along with *Alphonsus*, as Greene's answer to the successful *Tamburlaine*; he sees Greene taking the assumptions underlying the Marlovian hero and pushing them to their logical and absurd conclusion.[78] In his discussion of *Locrine* in *The English History Play*, Ribner points to the influence of Greene: "...we may perhaps most reasonably conclude that it is an earlier work by Robert Greene, parts of which he felt free to reuse in *Selimus*."[79] Ribner sees the characteristics of Greene's work first in the focus on the romance of battles and a love affair rather than on the historical aspect, second in the framework of dumb shows which is similar to that of *Alphonsus*, and third in the comic scenes with Strumbo which are reminiscent of those in Greene's prose works. While advocating Greene as the author of *Locrine*, Ribner adheres to the idea that *Locrine* is a revision of an older play. The most extensive study of *Locrine*, by Baldwin Maxwell in *Studies in the Shakespeare Apocrypha*, reaches the same conclusion, that *Locrine* is a revision and that the reviser also had a hand in the writing of *Selimus*; Maxwell tentatively points in the direction of Greene as author or reviser of both plays but does not press the point. In any case, he sees a complicated system of borrowing between the two plays in which *Selimus* borrows the Spenserian lines from *Locrine* and *Locrine* borrows the comic scene of Strumbo and Humber from Bullithrumble in *Selimus*. As well as this comic scene Maxwell believes that the meeting of Locrine and Estrild has been inserted into *Locrine*. These two scenes along with the character of Thrasimachus, who, as Maxwell points out, seems to become younger as the play progresses, and the inadequacy of the title, which describes only the first half of the action,[80] suggest that a revision of the original play has taken place.

Although critical opinion concerning the authorship of *Locrine* shows great diversity, one idea underlies many of the arguments--the present version of *Locrine* represents the work of at least two playwrights, one who wrote the original play and another who revised it. The statement on the title-page, "Newly set forth, overseen and corrected,/ By W.S.,"is not a great deal of help in the

---

[78]"Greene's Attack on Marlowe; Some Light on *Alphonsus* and *Selimus*," *Studies in Philology*, 52(1955), 162-171.

[79]Ribner discusses the authorship of *Locrine* on pp. 237-38.

[80]Similarly, Muriel C. Bradbrook ("Shakespeare and his Collaborators," *Shakespeare 1971*, ed. Clifford Leech and J.M.R. Margeson (Toronto: University of Toronto Press, 1972), p. 24) suggests that the first two acts of *Edward III*, concerning Edward's courtship of the Countess of Salisbury, are an addition because the title does not include them.

identification of the reviser, but we do know that the play was refurbished to some extent. The question arises as to the nature of the revisions--whether they were major, involving the construction of the play, or merely limited to a few lines in the epilogue. In the earlier discussion of the date of *Locrine* (p. 9), it was shown that the plot concerning Humber was altered to accommodate a comic scene. The fact that *Locrine* has been revised makes any attribution on the basis of style very uncertain; we are not dealing with the distinctive style of one man but with a collaboration between two, or even more.[81] The large number of borrowings, both of lines and dramatic techniques, do not prove that any one dramatist wrote the play, but, rather, that *Locrine* represents an attempt to include everything that had proven successful on the popular stage.

6. ATTRIBUTION TO COMPANY

Although we cannot determine the author of *Locrine*, the facts we do have--the entry in the Stationers' Register by Thomas Creede on July 20, 1594, and the close relationship with another of Creede's plays, *Selimus*, printed in 1594--point to a tentative attribution of *Locrine* to the Queen's Men. In *A Second Supplement to the Revised Edition* of *Annals of English Drama 975-1700*, Samuel Schoenbaum includes a note on *Locrine*. Under the category of "Auspices," which had originally read "Unknown" because of the lack of information on the title-page and the absence of any indication in the contemporary records, he suggests that we "read Queen's (?)" (p. 2). Schoenbaum suggests the likelihood of *Locrine* belonging to the Queen's Men on the strength of an article by G.M. Pinciss, "Thomas Creede and the Repertory of the Queen's Men, 1583-1592."[82] Pinciss has examined Creede's record of play publication and has found a correlation between the group of plays printed by Creede from 1594 to 1595 and the breaking-up of the Queen's Men as a London company and their subsequent going to the country to play. Henslowe has recorded in his *Diary* under "3 of maye 1593" that he loaned his nephew Francis Henslowe, a member of the Queen's Company, fifteen pounds when the Queen's Men "broke & went into the contrey to playe" (I,4); as Francis had been pawnbroking for his uncle throughout 1593 and until May 1594, Greg assumes that 1593 is an error and

---

[81] Samuel Schoenbaum (*Internal Evidence and Elizabethan Dramatic Authorship* (Evanston: Northwestern University Press, 1966), p. 168) points out that in order to analyze style the play must be written in a distinctive style, and "Collaborations...and revisions are less likely to manifest stylistic individuality than the unrevised work of a single author. The partners may adjust their styles to one another; the reviser may imitate his predecessor."

[82] *Modern Philology*, 67 (1969-70), 321-330.

INTRODUCTION 33

that the date should probably read 1594.[83] We can at least be reasonably sure that the Queen's Men ceased to exist as a London company. In the winter season of 1591-1592, there was only one performance at court as opposed to five during the previous season; in 1592-1593, the Queen's players did not perform at court at all, and on January 6, 1594 they gave their last royal performance.[84] The company continued to perform in London, however, until May of 1594; in the week April 1 to April 8, 1594 the Queen's Men performed with the Earl of Sussex's Men, probably at the Rose.[85] Two reasons for the break-up of the company are suggested by Chambers: either the plays in the Queen's repertory had ceased to be popular, or the company had been unable to bear the financial hardship of the plague years.[86] As the players jealously guarded their plays to protect them from piracy, and as they did not normally release them for publication while the plays were still drawing an audience, the fact that six plays with title-page attributions to the Queen's Men are entered in the Stationers' Register in little over a year, from May 14, 1594 to May 23, 1595, indicates both that the company needed to improve its finances and also that the players no longer wanted to perform on the London stages. The six plays are the following: *Friar Bacon* (entered in the Stationers' Register May 14, 1594 and printed in 1594); *King Leir* (entered May 14, 1594 and printed in 1605); *The Famous Victories* (entered May 14, 1594 and printed in 1598); *True Tragedy of Richard III* (entered June 19, 1594 and printed in 1594); *Old Wives' Tale* (entered April 16, 1595 and printed in 1595); *Valentine and Orson*, not extant (entered May 23, 1595). Two other plays not entered in the Stationers' Register, but with title-page attributions to the Queen's Men are *Selimus* (1594) and *Sir Clyomon and Sir Clamydes* (1599). Of the eight plays published belonging to the Queen's Men, four, *The Famous Victories*, *True Tragedy of Richard III*, *Selimus*, and *Sir Clyomon and Sir Clamydes*, were printed independently by Thomas Creede. Creede also printed five other plays[87] independently without any attribution to company: *The Looking-Glass* (entered in the Stationers' Register March 5, 1594 and printed in 1594); *The Pedlar's Prophecy* (entered May 13, 1594 and printed in 1595); *James IV* (entered May 14, 1594 and printed in 1598); *Locrine* (entered July 20, 1594 and printed in 1595); *Alphonsus* (printed in 1599 without a previous entry in the

---

[83]*Henslowe's Diary, Part II Commentary*, ed. W.W. Greg (London: A.H. Bullen, 1908), p. 277.

[84]Pinciss, "Thomas Creede," p. 321.

[85]John Tucker Murray, *English Dramatic Companies, 1558-1642* (New York: Russell & Russell, 1963), I, 13.

[86]*Elizabethan Stage*, II, 114.

[87]Chambers (*Elizabethan Stage*, III, 184, n.2) points out that a sixth play, *Menaechmi*, entered in the Stationers' Register June 10, 1594 and printed by Creede in 1595, was not an acting play.

the Stationers' Register). Of the nine plays printed
independently by Creede, seven were either printed or
entered in the Stationers' Register in 1594, the date of
the breaking-up of the Queen's Company. The suggestion
follows that Creede, who was just starting out in the
printing business, had made an arrangement with the
Queen's Men to print their plays, and that the five plays
with no attribution to company may have come, along with
the other four, from the Queen's Men.[88] There is other
evidence to support the association of *The Looking-Glass*,
James IV, *Alphonsus*, *The Pedlar's Prophecy* and *Locrine*
with the Queen's. The first three all indicate the
authorship of Robert Greene on their title-pages, and he
is associated with the Queen's Men through *Friar Bacon*,
attributed to the Queen's, and through the sale of another
of his plays, *Orlando Furioso*, to them. Pinciss, in his
discussion of the connection of Greene with the Queen's
Men, emphasizes that "none of Greene's plays can be
positively claimed for any acting company prior to their
ownership by the Queen's Men."[89] The intricate process of
borrowing between *Locrine* and *Selimus*, a Queen's play
printed in the same year that *Locrine* was entered in the
Stationers' Register, indicates that the author or reviser
of one play must have had access to the manuscript of the
other; it seems unlikely that the manuscript of a play
would be available to anyone outside the company.
Although the existing evidence suggests that *Locrine*
belonged to the Queen's Men, there is no record of a performance of the play in the late sixteenth or early
seventeenth centuries.[90]

7. TEXT

Thomas Creede printed *The Lamentable Tragedy of
Locrine* in 1595 sometime after November 17, the beginning
of the thirty-eighth year of Elizabeth's reign referred
to in the epilogue. The title-page reads as follows:

THE/ Lamentable Tragedie of/ *Locrine*, the eldest sonne
of King *Brutus*, discour-/ sing the warres of the
Britaines, and *Hunnes*,/ with their discomfiture:/ *The
Britaines victorie with their Accidents, and the/ death
of Albanact. No lesse pleasant then/ profitable./* Newly
set foorth, ouerseene and corrected,/ By W.S./ [printer's
device: McKerrow 299]/ LONDON/ Printed by Thomas Creede./
1595.

[88]*Ibid.*
[89]"Thomas Creede," pp. 328-329; further, Pinciss notes (p. 322)
that *The Pedlar's Prophecy* "may be ascribed to Robert Wilson," one of
the actors for the Queen's Men.
[90]The stage history comprises a single performance in London on
March 29, 1899 of a modern version of *Locrine* by Algernon C. Swinburne (*Who's Who in the Theatre*, 14th ed., p. 1422) in which the
popular Elizabethan elements of comedy and dumb show have been

The 1595 edition contains 40 unnumbered leaves with the collation A-K⁴. The first leaf is blank and the title-page is on A2ʳ. Creede's device shows Truth naked except for a crown being beaten by a heavenly hand holding a scourge; the motto reads "*Viressit Vulnere Veritas*."[91] The running-titles in *Locrine* are divided "*The lamentable Tragedie of Locrine*" (verso) and "*the eldest sonne of King Brutus*" (recto). A consistent pattern of variation shows that two sets of regularly alternating running-titles were used and, with the printing of D, those titles used to print the outer forme in sheets B and C were exchanged with those of the inner forme and vice versa.[92]

Creede's career as a printer began in 1593 with his first entry in the Stationers' Register. He established an office at the Catherine Wheel in Thames Street, and he continued to publish until he was succeeded in 1617 by Bernard Alsop, who had gone into partnership with Creede the year before.[93] The compositorial characteristics of all plays printed in Creede's shop between 1593 and 1602 have been examined and tabulated by George W. Williams.[94] In the plays printed in the first few years after Creede established his business, the evidence of spelling and typographical preferences point to the work of one compositor, possibly Creede himself. The spelling is characterized by a decided preference for "-ie" endings in nouns, adjectives and verbs, and for "-ly" endings in adverbs; in *Locrine*, a high proportion of "-ie" endings is evident (90%) with eight exceptions to the "-ly" ending. Spellings of the shorter words "bene," "do," and "here" occur with few variations in *Locrine* and are consistent with the other plays printed by Creede at this time. The typographical preferences in *Locrine* also reveal the work of one compositor: proper names are set in distinguishing type in stage directions and, with a few exceptions, in the text of the play; when the catch word indicates the beginning of a new speech, the speech prefix only is used rather than the speech prefix and the first word.

deleted in order to concentrate on Locrine's adulterous love affair.

[91]Williams observes ("Good Quarto of *Romeo and Juliet*," p. 7, n.10) that "The order of the three plays printed in 1595 can be partially determined by the deterioration of Creede's device on the title pages. The small line at the bottom center of the device appears in *Pedlars Prophecie* and *Menechmi* and plays of 1594 unbroken, and in *Locrine* and subsequent plays broken on the left side. It is thus evident that *Locrine* is the latest of the three. This order parallels the order of Register entry."

[92]See Williams' analysis of the running-titles, "Good Quarto of *Romeo and Juliet*," Chart 13, p. xvii, and his discussion of the interchange of skeletons in the printing of *Locrine*, pp. 30-31.

[93]R.B. McKerrow, ed., *A Dictionary of Printers and Booksellers* (London: Blades, East & Blades, 1910), pp. 80-81.

[94]"Good Quarto of *Romeo and Juliet*," Part I. See especially the discussion of *Locrine*, p. 31 and Chart 14, pp. xviii-xix. Williams summarizes his findings on p. 88.

On the basis of evidence afforded by the stage directions, it is reasonable to assume that the copy used to set the 1595 quarto was the author's or reviser's manuscript or a transcript of this. Most of the stage directions indicating entrances at the beginnings of scenes merely consist of "Enter" followed by a list of names. In some cases, however, the pattern is varied with the introduction of descriptive detail, and this is an indication of the author or reviser attempting to convey his impression of staging.[95] The stage directions for the comic subplot all appear to be of authorial origin: for example, location and descriptive qualifications are found in the stage direction "*Enter* STRUMBO *above, in a gown, with ink and paper in his hand, saying*" (I,iii). The stage direction describing Humber's entrance after his defeat gives specific details of his appearance, "*Enter* HUMBER *alone, his hair hanging over his shoulders, his arms all bloody, and a dart in one hand*" (IV,iii). Descriptive stage directions are confined generally to the comic episodes and the scene following Humber's defeat; these particular parts of *Locrine* may have been added later, and, thus, the stage directions would have been written by a reviser. One other piece of evidence which suggests an author's or reviser's manuscript rather than a theatrical prompt-book as the copy text is the presence of the ghost character Trussier. He enters with Humber's army (II,v) but is not assigned any speeches and does not have any function in the plot. W.W. Greg suggests that ghost characters probably are a characteristic of an authorial manuscript because the book-keeper in the theatre would undoubtedly remove such unnecessary names from his prompt-copy.[96]

An unusual feature of the thirteen extant copies of *Locrine*[97] is the complete lack of press variants. This does not mean necessarily that the play was uncorrected, but that the fourth stage of proofing, where the press is stopped in order to make corrections, has not been carried out. Corrections may have been made in the earlier stages of proofreading, in the manuscript, proofs and revises, for which we have no evidence.[98] Although the absence of press variants suggests continuous printing with no

---

[95]Sanders makes this point in his Introduction to *The Scottish History of James the Fourth* (London: Methuen, 1970), pp. lviii-lix.

[96]*The Shakespeare First Folio* (Oxford: Clarendon Press, 1955), p. 112.

[97]There are three copies in the British Library, two in the Folger (one is imperfect with A3, C1-D2, D4 and F1 lacking; the inner margins of some leaves have been repaired affecting some text), and single copies in the Bodleian, Pierpont Morgan, Trinity College, Cambridge, Birmingham Public, University of Illinois, Henry Huntington, Clark, UCLA and Bibliotheca Bodmeriana, Cologny, Geneva.

[98]Donald F. McKenzie, "Printers of the Mind," *Studies in Bibliography*, 22 (1969), 44-45.

concern for the correction of errors, the quality of printing in *Locrine* is good.[99]

The copy that the compositor was using was undoubtedly a good one because the majority of errors that require emendation are typographical and do not involve difficulties of sense. Emendations that are not merely corrections of typographical errors have been discussed in the commentary. A great deal of variation is seen in the speech prefixes, which have been normalized in this edition. A few stage directions are misplaced and many appear to be missing, but this could have been the fault of the copy. The play is regularly divided into acts and scenes; two of the scene divisions are obviously wrong.

Both the spelling and punctuation in this edition have been modernized. Colons used to indicate a pause or full-stop in the 1595 quarto have been replaced with commas and periods. Similarly, commas in the original edition that come at the end of a sentence have been replaced with periods. Many commas have been omitted where the sense does not require an end-stopped line. Proper names in the text which are distinguished by means of italics in the 1595 edition have been normalized. Capitalization has been brought into line with modern usage, and such words as "Iacinth," "Captaine," "King," "Maiestie," become in this edition "jacinth," "captain," "king," "majesty." The spelling has been modernized according to the suggestions of Stanley Wells in *Modernizing Shakespeare's Spelling*.[100] Genuine dialectal variants which are now obsolete have been retained; examples include nouns such as "gardiant," "inheritage," "mungrel," "occision"; adjectives such as "ybent," "unpartial," "unmoveable," "hugie," "masty"; verbs such as "rent" and "leese"; and the past tenses "drave," "stroke," "strooken," "strawed," "ware," and "spake." The particular uses of the words "squeltering" and "strangle" are unique in *Locrine*, and these archaic forms have been retained. The clown deliberately mispronounces words and, thus, normalization of his speech, for example with the words "Constultations" and "Antastick," would destroy some of the comic effect. Where appropriate "then" in the 1595 quarto has been given its modern equivalent "than." Contractions in the 1595 text have been expanded to the modern spelling where the modern equivalent does not produce a significant change in pronunciation or metre. The silent "e" omitted in words such as "lingring," "encountred," and "hastneth" before the "n" or "r" of the

---

[99]Williams ("Good Quarto of *Romeo and Juliet*," p. 88) considers the compositor responsible for the early plays, who may have been Creede himself, to be "...a careful and conscientious craftsman; his printing was clean and moderately accurate. His style and format were on a par with the better work of his contemporaries."

[100]This is published together with Gary Taylor's *Three Studies in the Text of Henry V* (Oxford: Clarendon Press, 1979).

inflexional ending has been replaced as the extra syllable would not significantly alter the sound of the word or the rhythm of the line. When inclusion of the "e" before the "st" ending in a word such as "camst" would change the metre of the line, then the modern equivalent is given with the apostrophe. Other examples of the modernization of spelling include "abhominable" being changed to "abominable," "sterve" to "starve," "vild" to "vile," "topace" to "topaz," and "murthered" to "murdered." Metrical markings are used to indicate pronunciation necessary for the metre of the line when that pronunciation differs from the modern one.

THE LAMENTABLE TRAGEDY OF LOCRINE

[*DRAMATIS PERSONAE*]

BRUTUS, king of Britain.
LOCRINE,
ALBANACT } sons to Brutus.
CAMBER,
MADAN, son to Locrine and Guendoline.
DEBON,
ASSARACUS, } followers of Brutus.
CORINEUS,
THRASIMACHUS, son to Corineus.
GHOST OF ALBANACT.
GHOST OF CORINEUS.
HUMBER, Scythian invader.
HUBBA, son to Humber.
SEGAR,
TRUSSIER, } followers of Humber.
STRUMBO, clown.
TROMPART, his man.
OLIVER, rustic.
WILLIAM, son to Oliver.
Captain, in Albanact's army.
Two Soliders.
Page.
Humber's Soldiers, Lords of Albany, Albanact's Soldiers,
    Locrine's Soldiers, Thrasimachus' Soldiers.
ATE, chorus.
GUENDOLINE, daughter to Corineus and wife to Locrine.

DRAMATIS PERSONAE] first given by Rowe (1709) and expanded by later editors. The above list is adapted from that given by McKerrow.

ESTRILD, wife to Humber.
SABREN, daughter to Estrild and Locrine.
DOROTHY, wife to Strumbo.
MARGERY, daughter to Oliver and wife to Strumbo.

Dumb Shows: I, Lion, Bear, Archer; II, Perseus, Cepheus, Andromeda, Phineus, Ethiopians; III, Crocodile, Snake; IV, Omphale, Hercules; V, Jason, Creon's Daughter, Medea.]

THE LAMENTABLE TRAGEDY OF LOCRINE,
THE ELDEST SON OF KING BRUTUS,

DISCOURSING THE WARS OF THE BRITONS AND HUNS,
WITH THEIR DISCOMFITURE, THE BRITONS' VICTORY
WITH THEIR ACCIDENTS, AND THE DEATH
OF ALBANACT.

ACT I

SCENE I

Enter ATE *with thunder and lightning, all in black, with a burning torch in one hand and a bloody sword in the other hand, and presently let there come forth a* Lion *running after a* Bear *or any other beast; then come forth an* Archer *who must kill the* Lion *in a dumb show, and then depart. Remain* ATE.

ATE. *In poenam sectatur et umbra.*
 A mighty lion, ruler of the woods,
 Of wondrous strength and great proportion,

The first Act.] *Q.* 0.1. ATE] *Pope*; Atey *Q.* 1. poenam] *Rowe*; paenam *Q.*

 0.1. ATE] "the name of a hurtefull spirite, alwaye woorkynge ill to men" (Cooper); cf. *John*, II,i,63: "An Ate, stirring him to... strife" (Onions). See Introduction, pp. 12-13. The quarto text also uses the spelling "Atey" at 11. 0.7 and 1.
 0.3. Lion] The king of beasts is an allegorical representation of King Brutus; similar animal symbolism is used in the pageants of genealogy (Venezky, *Pageantry*, p. 117).
 1.] "The ghost pursues for punishment" (Moltke); motto attached to Whitney's emblem (p. 32) depicting the terrors of conscience. See Introduction, p. 12.
 2.] Cf. Spenser, "Visions of the worlds vanitie," 1.127: "A mighty Lyon, Lord of all the wood"; see Introduction, p. 7.

With hideous noise scaring the trembling trees,
With yelling clamours shaking all the earth, 5
Traversed the groves, and chased the wand'ring beasts.
Long did he range amid the shady trees,
And drave the silly beasts before his face,
When suddenly from out a thorny bush
A dreadful archer with his bow ybent 10
Wounded the lion with a dismal shaft.
So he him stroke that it drew forth the blood,
And filled his furious heart with fretting ire;
But all in vain he threatneth teeth and paws,
And sparkleth fire from forth his flaming eyes, 15
For the sharp shaft gave him a mortal wound.
So valiant Brute, the terror of the world,
Whose only looks did scare his enemies,
The archer Death brought to his latest end.
O what may long abide above this ground 20
In state of bliss and healthful happiness? *Exit.*

---

4. scaring] *F*; scarring *Q*.

---

4. *scaring*] Although the play uses a great deal of hyperbolic language, the sense of the line seems to require the F reading of "scaring" rather than the Q reading of "scarring"; similarly at I,ii,77.
8. *silly*] "defenceless"; "deserving of pity" (*O.E.D.*, adj., 1.a and b).
11. *dismal*] fatal.
12. *stroke*] obsolete past tense and past participle of "strike" (*O.E.D.*).
12-15.] Cf. "Visions of the worlds vanitie," 11.135-38:
Sore he him stong, that it the blood forth drawes,
And his proude heart is fild with fretting ire:
In vaine he threats his teeth, his tayle, his pawes,
And from his bloodie eyes doth sparkle fire.
15. *from forth*] normal order inverted for emphasis.
18.] Cf. *Selimus*, 1.181: "Whose onely name affrights your enemies" (Hubbard, "*Locrine* and *Selimus*," p. 28).
20-21.] Cf. Spenser, "The Ruines of Time," 11.568-69:
"But what can long abide aboue this ground/ In state of blis, or stedfast happinesse?"

SC. II] TRAGEDY OF LOCRINE 45

SCENE II

Enter BRUTUS *carried in a chair*, LOCRINE, CAMBER, ALBANACT, CORINEUS, GUENDOLINE, ASSARACUS, DEBON, THRASIMACHUS.

Brut. Most loyal lords and faithful followers,
 That have with me, unworthy general,
 Passèd the greedy gulf of Ocean,
 Leaving the confines of fair Italy,
 Behold, your Brutus draweth nigh his end, 5
 And I must leave you, though against my will.
 My sinews shrunk, my numbèd senses fail,
 A chilling cold possesseth all my bones;
 Black ugly Death, with visage pale and wan,
 Presents himself before my dazzled eyes, 10
 And with his dart preparèd is to strike.
 These arms, my lords, these never daunted arms,
 That oft have quelled the courage of my foes,
 And eke dismayed my neighbours' arrogance,
 Now yield to death, o'erlaid with crooked age, 15
 Devoid of strength and of their proper force,
 Even as the lusty cedar worn with years

0.2. CORINEUS] *M*; Corineius *Q*. 0.2. GUENDOLINE] *This ed.*; Guendelin *Q*. 14. arrogance] *F*; arrogancie *Q*.

---

3. *Ocean*] "great god of the sea, and father of al the ryuers" (Cooper).
7.] reminiscent of King Charles' dying words in Marlowe's *The Massacre at Paris*, "...my sight begins to fail,/ My sinews shrink..." (xiii,13-14); also, a parallel is found in Peele's *The Old Wives Tale*, 1.812: "Alas my vaines are numbd, my sinews shrinke."
8.] Cf. *Selimus*, 1.1250: "Me thinkes I feele a cold run through my bones."
9.] Death was often represented as a figure draped in black with a skeletal face.
9-11.] similar to the approach of Death in *Tamburlaine, Part II*, V,iii,67-69; cf. Peele, "Tale of Troy," 1.445: "With slaughtring hand, with visage pale and grim" (W.S. Gaud, "The Authorship of *Locrine*," *Modern Philology*, 1 (1904), 421).
12.] This type of repetition is relatively rare, occurring in *Locrine*, *1H6* and the plays of Peele (Hubbard, "Repetition and Parallelism," p. 363).
16. *proper*] own.

> That far abroad her dainty odour throws
> 'Mongst all the daughters of proud Lebanon.
> This heart, my lords, this ne'er appallèd heart,   20
> That was a terror to the bord'ring lands,
> A doleful scourge unto my neighbour kings,
> Now by the weapons of unpartial death
> Is clove asunder and bereft of life,
> As when the sacred oak with thunderbolts   25
> Sent from the fiery circuit of the heavens,
> Sliding along the air's celestial vaults,
> Is rent and cloven to the very roots.
> In vain, therefore, I strangle with this foe;
> Then welcome, death, since God will have it so.   30
> *Assar.* Alas, my lord, we sorrow at your case,
> And grieve to see your person vexèd thus,
> But whatsoe'er the Fates determined have,
> It lieth not in us to disannul;
> And he that would annihilate his mind,   35
> Soaring with Icarus too near the sun,
> May catch a fall with young Bellerophon.
> For when the fatal sisters have decreed

29. strangle] *Q*; struggle *F*.

18-19.] Cf. "Visions of the worlds vanitie," 11.87-88: "That farre abroad her daintie odours threwe;/ Mongst all the daughers of proud Libanon."
    23. *unpartial*] obsolete form of "impartial" which was "very common from c. 1590 to c. 1660" (*O.E.D.*, *a.*, 1.a).
    25. *sacred oak*] sacred tree of Zeus.
    29. *strangle*] "To be at close grips, to struggle *with*"; according to the *O.E.D.* (*v.*, 1.d, *intr.*), *Locrine* contains the sole instance of "strangle" in this sense. The Folio editor (1664) adopts the modern form "struggle."
    33. *Fates*] three sisters: Clotho, the spinner; Lachesis, the measurer; and Atropos, the one who cuts the thread of life.
    34. *disannul*] cancel; cf. *Err.*, I,i,145: "Our Lawes...Which Princes, would they, may not disanull" (*O.E.D.*, *v.*, 1., *trans.*).
    35-36.] He who thinks that he can defy physical law will, like Icarus, destroy himself; for the story of Icarus, see Ovid, *The Metamorphoses*, trans. Horace Gregory (New York: New American Library of World Literature, 1960), VIII.
    37. *Bellerophon*] attempted to fly to Olympus on the winged horse Pegasus but was thrown to the earth.
    38. *fatal sisters*] see note 1.33.

SC. II]   TRAGEDY OF LOCRINE   47

    To separate us from this earthly mould,
    No mortal force can countermand their minds.   40
    Then, worthy lord, since there's no way but one,
    Cease your laments, and leave your grievous moan.
Cor. Your highness knows how many victories,
    How many trophies I erected have
    Triumphantly in every place we came.   45
    The Grecian monarch, warlike Pandrassus,
    And all the crew of the Molossians,
    Goffarius, the arm-strong king of Gauls,
    And all the borders of great Aquitaine
    Have felt the force of our victorious arms,   50
    And to their cost beheld our chivalry.
    Where'er Aurora, handmaid of the sun,
    Where'er the sun-bright guardiant of the day,
    Where'er the joyful day with cheerful light,
    Where'er the light illuminates the world,   55
    The Trojans' glory flies with golden wings,
    Wings that do soar beyond fell envious flight.
    The fame of Brutus and his followers
    Pierceth the skies, and with the skies, the throne
    Of might Jove, commander of the world.   60

40. mortal] *F*; mortalll *Q*. 52. Aurora] *Rowe*; Ancora *Q*. 55. world] *F*; word *Q*.

---

  43. *victories*] triumphs; personified by statues of the Roman goddess Victory (*O.E.D.*, *sb.*, 3 and 4).
  44. *trophies*] monuments.
  46. *Pandrassus*] held the descendants of Helenus (son of Priam) in bondage until they were freed by Brutus.
  47. *Molossians*] people living in north-western Greece.
  48. *Goffarius*] Goffarius Pictus, whose army was defeated when Brutus invaded Aquitaine.
  49. *Aquitaine*] province of central and south-western France.
  51. *chivalry*] "Knights or horsemen equipped for battle" (*O.E.D.*, 1. *collect*).
  52-55.] rhetorical figure, "anaphora" or "report," when one word begins several lines in succession (George Puttenham, *The Arte of English Poesie*, ed. Gladys Doidge Willcock and Alice Walker (Cambridge: Cambridge University Press, 1936), Bk. III, chap. xix).
  52. *Aurora*] goddess of early morning.
  53. *guardiant*] "guardian" (*O.E.D.*, *Obs. rare*).

48   TRAGEDY OF LOCRINE   [ACT I

    Then, worthy Brutus, leave these sad laments;
    Comfort yourself with this your great renown,
    And fear not Death though he seem terrible.
Brut. Nay, Corineus, you mistake my mind
    In construing wrong the cause of my complaints.   65
    I feared to yield myself to fatal death!
    God knows it was the least of all my thought;
    A greater care torments my very bones,
    And makes me tremble at the thought of it,
    And in you, lordings, doth the substance lie.   70
Thra. Most noble lord, if aught your loyal peers
    Accomplish may, to ease your lingering grief,
    I, in the name of all, protest to you
    That we will boldly enterprise the same,
    Were it to enter to black Tartarus   75
    Where triple Cerberus with his venomous throat
    Scareth the ghosts with high-resounding noise.
    We'll either rent the bowels of the earth,
    Searching the entrails of the brutish earth,
    Or with his Ixion's over-daring son,   80
    Be bound in chains of ever-during steel.
Brut. Then hearken to your sovereign's latest words,
    In which I will unto you all unfold
    Our royal mind and resolute intent:

64. Corineus] *M*; Corinus *Q*. 67. God] *F*; Cod *Q*. 77. Scareth] *F*; Scarreth *Q*. 80. son] *M*; soone *Q*.

---

    65. *wrong*] In the late 16th and early 17th centuries, it was common for adjectives to be used as adverbs; cf. *Shr.*, I,i,89: "Thou didst it excellent" (Abbott, sec. 1).
    74. *enterprise*] undertake.
    75. *Tartarus*] hell.
    76. *triple Cerberus*] "A dogge with three heades, whiche...was porter of hell..." (Cooper).
    78. *rent*] obsolete (except dialectal) form of "rend" (*O.E.D.*, v.^{2}, 1. trans.).
    80. *his Ixion's*] repetition of the possessive; perhaps should read Ixion's his; see Abbott, sec. 217.
    80. *son*] Pirithous, a centaur.

SC. II]   TRAGEDY OF LOCRINE   49

    When golden Hebe, daughter to great Jove,   85
    Covered my manly cheeks with youthful down,
    Th'unhappy slaughter of my luckless sire
    Drove me and old Assaracus, mine eme,
    As exiles from the bounds of Italy,
    So that perforce we were constrained to fly   90
    To Grecians' monarch, noble Pandrassus.
    There I alone did undertake your cause;
    There I restored your antique liberty,
    Though Grecia frowned, and all Molossia stormed;
    Though brave Antigonus with martial band   95
    In pitchèd field encountered me and mine;
    Though Pandrassus and his contributories,
    With all the rout of their confederates,
    Sought to deface our glorious memory
    And wipe the name of Trojans from the earth;   100
    Him did I captivate with this mine arm,
    And by compulsion forced him to agree
    To certain articles which there we did propound.
    From Grecia through the boisterous Hellespont,
    We came unto the fields of Lestrigon,   105

88. Assaracus] *Hazlitt*; Assarachus *Q*.

---

  85. *Hebe*] goddess of adolescence.
  87.] Brutus mistook his father for a deer while hunting and, thus, fulfilled a prophecy that he would kill his father (*Historia*, I,iii).
  88. *Assaracus*] ally of Brutus in the struggle against Pandrassus; in the *Historia* (I,iii), Brutus meets Assaracus in Greece.
  88. *eme*] uncle; later, Assaracus is referred to as the brother of Brutus: V,ii,9 and V,ii,86.
  95. *Antigonus*] brother of Pandrassus.
  96. *pitchèd field*] battle-ground.
  97. *contributories*] those who are tributary to Pandrassus either by supplying aid or by paying tribute.
  105. *Lestrigon*] southern Italy; home of the Lestrygones, "people in the extréeme parte of Italy...which dyd eate the companions of Uliûes..." (Cooper).

Whereas our brother Corineus was.
Which when we passèd the Sicilian gulf,
And so transfretting the Illyrian sea,
Arrivèd on the coasts of Aquitaine,
Where with an army of his barbarous Gauls,   110
Goffarius and his brother Gathelus
Encountering with our host, sustained the foil.
And for your sakes my Turnus there I lost,
Turnus that slew six hundred men-at-arms
All in an hour, with his sharp battle-axe.   115
From thence upon the strands of Albion
To Corus' haven happily we came,
And quelled the giants, come of Albion's race,
With Gogmagog, son to Samotheus,
The cursèd captain of that damnèd crew;   120
And in that isle at length I placèd you.
Now let me see if my laborious toils,

106. Corineus] *M*; Corineius *Q*. 107. Which] *Q*; Since *M*. 107. Sicilian] *Pope*; Cicillian *Q*. 108. Illyrian] *M*; Illician *Q*. 116. strands] *Simms*; strons *Q*. 118. come] *F*; comne *Q*.

---

106. *Whereas*] where; cf. *2H6*, I,ii,57-58: "Unto St. Alban's,/ Whereas the king and queen do mean to hawk" (Abbott, sec. 116).
106.] Corineus, an exile from Troy, settled with his followers on the shores of the Tyrrhene Sea (*Historia*, I,xii).
107. *Which*] The emendation "Since" suggested by Malone is more plausible in the context, but it is unlikely that "Which" is a compositor error.
108. *transfretting*] crossing; *Locrine* cited by the *O.E.D.* (v. *Obs.*, 2. *trans.*, b.).
108. *Illyrian sea*] probably corresponds to what is now known as the Adriatic Sea; Illyria comprised almost the same area as Yugoslavia.
111. *Gathelus*] not found in any source (Erbe, "Die Locrinesage," p. 65).
112. *sustained the foil*] i.e., suffered defeat.
113. *Turnus*] nephew of Brutus after whom Tours was named; see Introduction, p. 2, n. 6.
114-115.] Cf. *Historia*, I,xv: "He with his single sword slew no less than six hundred men."
116. *Albion*] former name of Britain, after a giant, son of Neptune.
117. *Corus*] west wind (Cooper).
119. *Gogmagog*] a giant thrown off a cliff into the sea by Corineus.
119. *son to Samotheus*] This relationship is not found in any source (Erbe, "Die Locrinesage," pp. 65-66).

SC. II] TRAGEDY OF LOCRINE 51

  If all my care, if all my grievous wounds,
  If all my diligence were well employed.
Cor. When first I followed thee and thine, brave king, 125
  I hazarded my life and dearest blood
  To purchase favour at your princely hands,
  And for the same in dangerous attempts,
  In sundry conflicts and in divers broils,
  I showed the courage of my manly mind. 130
  For this I combated with Gathelus,
  The brother to Goffarius of Gaul;
  For this I fought with furious Gogmagog,
  A savage captain of a savage crew;
  And for these deeds brave Cornwall I received, 135
  A grateful gift given by a gracious king;
  And for this gift, this life and dearest blood
  Will Corineus spend for Brutus' good.
Deb. And what my friend, brave prince, hath vowed to you,
  The same will Debon do unto his end. 140
Brut. Then, loyal peers, since you are all agreed,
  And resolute to follow Brutus' hosts,
  Favour my sons, favour these orphans, lords,
  And shield them from the dangers of their foes.
  Locrine, the column of my family 145
  And only pillar of my weakened age,
  Locrine, draw near, draw near unto thy sire,
  And take thy latest blessings at his hands.
  And, for thou art the eldest of my sons,
  Be thou a captain to thy bretheren 150
  And imitate thy agèd father's steps,
  Which will conduct thee to true honour's gate;
  For if thou follow sacred virtue's lore,

142. hosts] *Rowe*; hoasts *Q*; hests *M*.

---

 145. *column*] support.
 149. *for*] because; also, 1.153 (Abbott, sec. 151).
 150. *bretheren*] This variant spelling of "brethren" is retained as it indicates pronunciation for rhythm.

Thou shalt be crownèd with a laurel branch
And wear a wreath of sempiternal fame,   155
Sorted amongst the glorious happy ones.

Loc. If Locrine do not follow your advice,
And bear himself in all things like a prince
That seeks to amplify the great renown
Left unto him for an inheritage   160
By those that were his ancestors,
Let me be flung into the ocean,
And swallowed in the bowels of the earth,
Or let the ruddy lightning of great Jove
Descend upon this my devolted head.   165

    BRUTUS *taking* GUENDOLINE *by the hand.*

Brut. But for I see you all to be in doubt
Who shall be matchèd with our royal son,
Locrine, receive this present at my hand,
A gift more rich than are the wealthy mines
Found in the bowels of America.   170
Thou shalt be spousèd to fair Guendoline;
Love her and take her, for she is thine own,
If so thy uncle and herself do please.

Cor. And herein how your highness honours me
It cannot be in my speech expressed,   175
For careful parents glory not so much
At their honour and promotion,

165. devolted] *Q*; devoted *Rowe*.   177. their honour] *Q*; their own honour *M*.

---

    156. *Sorted*] "chosen" (*O.E.D.*, *ppl.a.*, 1).
    162. *ocean*] trisyllabic here.
    165. *devolted*] bowed; obsolete form of "devolve" meaning "to roll down" or "cause to descend" (*O.E.D.*, *v.*, 1). Rowe's emendation "devoted" is plausible, but Q is not impossible.
    169-170. *wealthy...America*] Cf. *Tamburlaine*, Part II, I,iii,35: "Fraughted with gold of rich America" (Dean B. Lyman, Jr., "Apocryphal Plays of the University Wits," *English Studies in Honor of James Southall Wilson*, ed. Fredson Bowers (Charlottesville: University of Virginia, 1951), p. 218).
    176-179.] ulterior motives of Corineus are emphasized in *The Mirror For Magistrates*, "Locrinus," 11.31-35.
    177. *their honour*] Malone's suggested emendation to improve the rhythm of the line by adding "own" is interesting but conjectural.

	As for to see the issue of their blood	
	Seated in honour and prosperity.	
Guen.	And far be it from my maiden's thoughts	180
	To contradict her agèd father's will.	
	Therefore, since he to whom I must obey	
	Hath given me now unto your royal self,	
	I will not stand aloof from off the lure,	
	Like crafty dames that most of all deny	185
	That which they most desire to possess.	

BRUTUS *turning to* LOCRINE.
LOCRINE *kneeling.*

Brut.	Then now, my son, thy part is on the stage,	
	For thou must bear the person of a king.	

Puts the crown on his head.

	Locrine, stand up and wear the regal crown,	
	And think upon the state of majesty,	190
	That thou with honour well mayst wear the crown;	
	And if thou tend'rest these my latest words,	
	As thou requir'st my soul to be at rest,	
	As thou desir'st thine own security,	
	Cherish and love thy new-betrothèd wife.	195
Loc.	No longer let me well enjoy the crown,	
	Than I do peerless Guendoline.	
Brut.	Camber.	
Cam.	My lord.	
Brut.	The glory of mine age	

197. do peerless] *Q*; do honour peerlesse *M*.

---

184. *lure*] bait used by a falconer to train the bird to return.
187-188. *thy...king*] Brutus is referring to the universal drama of life where Locrine must take the role of king (Anne Righter, *Shakespeare and the Idea of the Play* (London: Chatto & Windus, 1962), p. 136).
192. *tend'rest*] "to attend to or comply with (a request) graciously" (*O.E.D.*, Tender, $v.^2$ arch. or *dial.*, 3b).
197. *do peerless*] The line seems unusually short and a word may have been omitted which would have completed the parallelism with the previous line; Malone makes the interesting suggestion that the line be emended to "do honour peerless."

54   TRAGEDY OF LOCRINE   [ACT I

        And darling of thy mother Innogen,
        Take thou the South for thy dominion.   200
        From thee there shall proceed a royal race,
        That shall maintain the honour of this land,
        That sway the regal sceptre with their hands.
                                Turning to ALBANACT.
        And Albanact, thy father's only joy,
        Youngest in years, but not the youngest in mind, 205
        A perfect pattern of all chivalry,
        Take thou the North for thy dominion,
        A country full of hills and raggèd rocks,
        Replenishèd with fierce untamèd beasts,
        As correspondent to thy martial thoughts.   210
        Live long, my sons, with endless happiness,
        And bear firm concordance amongst yourselves.
        Obey the counsels of these fathers grave
        That you may better bear out violence.
        But suddenly, through weakness of my age   215
        And the defect of youthful puissance,
        My malady increaseth more and more,
        And cruel Death hasteneth his quickened pace
        To dispossess me of my earthly shape;

199. Innogen] *corr. Th*; Iunoger *Q.*   203. That] *Q*; And *Rowe.*   204.
only] *Simms*; onely *Q*; other *Moltke.*   205. Youngest] *F*; Yoongst *Q.*

    199. *Innogen*] daughter of Pandrassus; in exchange for the life of
Pandrassus, Brutus demanded Innogen for his wife.
    202.] division of the kingdom; see Introduction, pp. 24-25.
    203. *That*] The emendation of the quarto text to "And," suggested
by Rowe, is plausible because the compositor may have repeated the
initial "That" of the previous line by mistake; however, the emendation would change the meaning slightly.
    204. *only*] Moltke suggests the emendation "other"; "only" does
have the meaning, however, of peerless or pre-eminent and in this
sense fits into this context, even though Locrine and Camber also
give Brutus joy.
    210. *correspondent*] suitable or agreeable.
    214. *bear out*] sustain or endure.
    216. *defect*] lack or absence.
    218.] see note 11.9-11.

SC. II]   TRAGEDY OF LOCRINE   55

    Mine eyes wax dim, overcast with clouds of age;   220
    The pangs of death compass my crazèd bones.
    Thus to you all my blessings I bequeath,
    And with my blessings, this my fleeting soul.
    My glass is run, and all my miseries
    Do end with life; death closeth up mine eyes,   225
    My soul in haste flies to the Elysian fields.
                                            He dieth.

Loc. Accursèd stars, damned and accursèd stars,
    To abbreviate my noble father's life!
    Hard-hearted gods, and too envious Fates,
    Thus to cut off my father's fatal thread!   230
    Brutus, that was a glory to us all,
    Brutus, that was a terror to his foes,
    Alas, too soon by Demogorgon's knife,
    The martial Brutus is bereft of life.

Cor. No sad complaints may move just Aeacus;   235
    No dreadful threats can fear judge Rhadamanth.
    Wert thou as strong as mighty Hercules
    That tamed the hugie monsters of the world,

233. Demogorgon's] *Hazlitt;* Demagorgons *Q.* 235. (prefix) *Cor.*] corr. *Simms;* precedes 236 *Q.* 235. Aeacus] *Pope;* Lacus *Q.* 236. Rhadamanth] *M;* Rhodomanth *Q.*

---

221. *crazèd*] infirm.
224. *glass*] in a figurative sense, the hour-glass measuring the length of his life.
226. *Elysian fields*] "A place of pleasure, where poetes did suppose the soules of good men to dwell" (Cooper).
229-230. *too...thread*] see note 1.33.
233. *Demogorgon*] Cf. *Orlando Furioso* (printed quarto), 1.1279: "...*Demogorgon qui noctis fata gubernas*" (see Baldwin, *Literary Genetics*, pp. 70-72).
235. *Aeacus*] a judge in hell along with Minos and Rhadamanth (1.238).
236. *fear*] i.e., frighten; cf. *3H6*,III,iii,226: "Thou seest what's past; go fear thy king withal" (Abbott, sec. 291).
238. *hugie*] used by poets of the 16th century, apparently to create a dissyllable in the line of poetry; cf. *Selimus*, 1.1768: "Like hugie mountaines do your waters reare" (Howard Baker, *Induction to Tragedy* (New York: Russell & Russell, 1965), pp. 17, 63-8).

TRAGEDY OF LOCRINE   [ACT I

    Play'dst thou as sweet on the sweet sounding lute
    As did the spouse of fair Eurydice,   240
    That did enchant the waters with his noise,
    And made stones, birds and beasts to lead a dance,
    Constrained the hilly trees to follow him,
    Thou couldst not move the judge of Erebus,
    Nor move compassion in grim Pluto's heart;   245
    For fatal Mors expecteth all the world,
    And every man must tread the way of death.
    Brave Tantalus, the valiant Pelops' sire,
    Guest to the gods, suffered untimely death,
    And old Tithonus, husband to the morn,   250
    And eke grim Minos, whom just Jupiter
    Deigned to admit unto his sacrifice.
    The thundering trumpets of blood-thirsty Mars,
    The fearful rage of fell Tisiphone,
    The boisterous waves of humid Ocean   255

---

240. Eurydice] *M*; Euridies *Q*.   244. Erebus] *Rowe*; Crebus *Q*.
250. Tithonus] *Rowe*; Fleithonus *Q*.

   239-243.] see Ovid, *Metamorphoses*, X.
   241. *noise*] music.
   244. *Erebus*] region of hell.
   245. *Pluto*] god of the underworld.
   246.] Death, an infernal deity, waits for all men in the sense that death is in store for everyone.
   248-249.] After attending an Olympian banquet, Tantalus betrayed the counsel of the gods; his punishment in hell consisted of standing beside a river and an apple tree both of which just eluded his grasp.
   248. *Pelops*] won Hippodameia, daughter of Oenomaus, by bribing Myrtilus, Oenomaus' charioteer, to remove the linchpins from Oenomaus' chariot, and Oenomaus was subsequently killed (*O.C.D.*).
   250. *Tithonus*] His wife, Eos, begged Zeus to make him immortal, but forgot to ask for eternal youth (Michael Grant, *Myths of the Greeks and Romans* (Toronto: New American Library of Canada, 1962), p. 393).
   251-252.] Poseidon sent Minos a bull to sacrifice, thus confirming his claim to the kingship; but he did not sacrifice the bull because it was so handsome, and his wife, Pasiphae, fell in love with it, producing the Minotaur (Grant, *Myths*, p. 339).
   254. *Tisiphone*] The three furies were Tisiphone, Alecto and Megaera; they avenged crimes by pursuing the culprits relentlessly.

SC. II]   TRAGEDY OF LOCRINE   57

    Are instruments and tools of dismal death.
    Then, noble cousin, cease to mourn his chance,
    Whose age and years were signs that he should die.
    It resteth now that we inter his bones,
    That was a terror to his enemies.   260
    Take up the corse and, princes, hold him dead,
    Who while he lived, upheld the Trojan state.
    Sound drums and trumpets; march to Troynovant,
    There to provide our chieftain's funeral.   [*Exeunt.*]

SCENE III

Enter STRUMBO *above, in a gown, with ink and*
paper in his hand, saying,

Strum. Either the four elements, the seven planets and
    all the particular stars of the pole Antastick, are
    adversative against me, or else I was begotten and
    born in the wane of the moon, when everything, as
    saith Lactantius in his fourth book of Consulta-   5

264. *Exeunt.*] *F.*

---

  257. *cousin*] Corineus is referred to as the uncle of Locrine at
III,ii,80 and IV,ii,162; but cousin is used in the more general sense
of kinsman.
  263. *Troynovant*] new Troy, the capital of Britain; see Introduction, p. 23.
  I.iii.0.1. *above*] balcony over the stage; the descriptive quality
of this stage direction suggests authorial origin. See Introduction,
p. 36.
  1. *seven planets*] The Ptolemaic system accounted for the motions
of seven planets about the earth--the moon, Mercury, Venus, Sun, Mars,
Jupiter, Saturn.
  2. *Antastick*] comic perversion of Antarctic.
  5. *Lactantius...Constultations*] Lactantius, a teacher of Latin
rhetoric at Nicomedia early in the fourth century A.D., is remembered
for his defense of Christianity; his best known work is the *Divine*
Institutes in seven books (Shirley Jackson Case, *Makers of Christianity From Jesus to Charlemagne* (Port Washington, New York: Kennikat
Press, 1971), pp. 109-114). He is not known to have written *Consultations*, and Strumbo may have invented the title in order to capitalize
on the malapropism with its hidden pun on stultification.

tions doth say, goeth arseward. Ay, masters, ay, you
may laugh, but I must weep; you may joy, but I must
sorrow; shedding salt tears from the wat'ry fountains
of my most dainty fair eyes, along my comely and
smooth cheeks, in as great plenty as the water   10
runneth from the bucking-tubs, or red wine out of
the hogsheads. For trust me, gentlemen and my very
good friends, and so forth, the little god, nay the
desperate god Cuprit, with one of his vengible bird-
bolts, hath shot me unto the heel; so not only,   15
but also, O fine phrase, I burn, I burn, and I burn-
a, in love, in love, and in love-a. Ah, Strumbo, what
hast thou seen? not Dina with the Ass Tom? Yea, with
these eyes thou hast seen her, and therefore pull
them out, for they will work thy bale. Ah,   20
Strumbo, hast thou heard? not the voice of the
nightingale, but a voice sweeter than hers; yea,
with these ears hast thou heard them, and therefore
cut them off, for they have caused thy sorrow. Nay,

I.iii.6. arseward] *Hazlitt*; asward *Q*; arsward *F*. 21. hast] *Q*; what hast *M*. 23. them] *Q*; it *M*.

---

11. *bucking-tubs*] wash-tubs; name derived from the buck or lye used (Onions).
12. *hogsheads*] large casks for liquor.
14. *Cuprit*] Cupid, with a pun on "culprit."
14. *vengible*] vengeful.
14-15. *bird-bolts*] blunt-headed arrows used to shoot birds (Onions).
15-16. *not...phrase*] Strumbo is poking fun at the flowery language of Euphuism.
16-17. *I...burn-a*] Cf. Pyrochles in *The Faerie Queene*, II,vi,44: "I burne, I burne, I burne."
18. *Dina...Tom*] probably an allusion to Diana and Acteon (Ovid, *Metamorphoses*, III).
18.] Malone suggests that a phrase--"but one more beautiful than her"--has been omitted after "Tom," but the text does not require such an addition.
20. *work...bale*] cause trouble for you.
21. *hast*] Malone makes the interesting suggestion that "what" should precede "hast" in order to complete the parallelism with 1.17, but the quarto is sufficient.
23. *them*] Malone's suggested emendation "it" is more logical, but the quarto reading is not impossible.

SC. III]   TRAGEDY OF LOCRINE   59

>   Strumbo, kill thyself, drown thyself, hang thyself,   25
>   starve thyself. O, but then I shall leave my sweet-
>   heart. O my heart! Now, pate, [*Scratching his head.*]
>   for thy master! I will dite an aliquant love-pistle
>   to her, and then she, hearing the grand verbosity of
>   my scripture, will love me presently. *Let him*   30
>   *write a little and then read.* My pen is naught;
>   gentlemen, lend me a knife. [*Sharpens pen.*] I
>   think the more haste the worst speed. *Then write*
>   *again, and after read.*
>   So it is, Mistress Dorothy, and the sole   35
>   essence of my soul, that the little sparkles of
>   affection kindled in me towards your sweet self hath
>   now increased to a great flame, and will, ere it be
>   long, consume my poor heart, except you with the
>   pleasant water of your secret fountain, quench   40
>   the furious heat of the same. Alas, I am a gentle-

27. *Scratching his head.*] Moltke.   32. *Sharpens pen.*] This ed.

---

  28. *dite*] compose.
  28. *aliquant*] eloquent; there may also be a play on the word "alicant," which refers to a kind of wine of a deep red colour made at Alicante in Spain. A similar play on words occurs in *Wiv.*, II,ii, 69, when Mistress Quickly speaks of "alligant terms."
  30. *scripture*] writing.
  31-32. *My...knife*] "Str. here, and in many other places in this play, addresses the groundlings, for whose entertainment alone he seems to have been introduced" (Malone).
  32-33. *I...speed*] proverbial; *Locrine* cited by Tilley, H198.
  36-41. *little...same*] The idea of the "secret fountain"--although a commonplace--may have been influenced by *Soliman and Perseda*, in which an elaborate conceit is used to express realistic desire:
    Brests, like two ouerflowing Fountaines,
    Twixt which a vale leads to the Elisian shades,
    Where vnder couert lyes the fount of pleasure
    Which thoughts may gesse, but tongue must not prophane.
                                                    (IV,i,84-87)
Baldwin notes the occurrence of this conceit in *Literary Genetics*, pp. 219-20. Similarly, the literal meaning of Venus' invitation to Adonis in Shakespeare's poem is camouflaged with a pastoral conceit:
    I'll be a park, and thou shalt be my deer:
    Feed where thou wilt, on mountain or in dale;
       Graze on my lips, and if those hills be dry,
       Stray lower, where the pleasant fountains lie. (11.231-34)
Steevens (1780) noted the parallel with *Locrine*.

man of good fame and name, majestical, in 'parel
comely, in gait portly. Let not therefore your
gentle heart be so hard as to despise a proper tall
young man of a handsome life, and by despising   45
him, not only, but also to kill him. Thus expecting
time and tide, I bid you farewell.

       Your servant,
        Signior Strumbo

O wit! O pate! O memory! O hand! O ink! O   50
paper! Well, now I will send it away. Trompart,
Trompart! What a villain is this? Why, sirrah,
come when your master calls you. Trompart!

    TROMPART *entering saith,*

Trom. Anon, Sir.

Strum. Thou knowest, my pretty boy, what a good   55
  master I have been to thee ever since I took thee
  into my service.

Trom. Ay, Sir.

Strum. And how I have cherished thee always, as if you
  had been the fruit of my loins, flesh of my flesh 60
  and bone of my bone.

Trom. Ay, Sir.

Strum. Then show thyself herein a trusty servant, and
  carry this letter to Mistress Dorothy, and tell her--
        Speaking in his ear.
        Exit TROMPART.

Nay, masters, you shall see a marriage by-and-by.   65
But here she comes. Now must I frame my amorous
passions.

42. fame and name, majestical,] *Hazlitt*; fame, and name,
maiesticall, *Q*.

---

 42. *'parel*] apparel.
 46. *not...also*] see note 1.14.
 49. *Signior*] a corruption of the Italian "*signore.*"
 51. *Trompart*] name of Braggadocchio's man in *The Faerie Queene*
(II,iii,10); see Introduction, p. 4.
 66. *frame*] shape, give expression to.

SC. III]   TRAGEDY OF LOCRINE   61

                    Enter DOROTHY *and* TROMPART.

Dor. Signior Strumbo, well met. I received your letters
    by your man here, who told me a pitiful story of
    your anguish, and so understanding your passions   70
    were so great, I came hither speedily.
Strum. O my sweet and pigsney, the fecundity of my
    ingeny is not so great that may declare unto you
    the sorrowful sobs and broken sleeps that I suffered
    for your sake; and therefore I desire you to   75
    receive me into your familiarity.
            For your love doth lie
            As near and as nigh
            Unto my heart within,
            As mine eye to my nose,   80
            My leg unto my hose,
            And my flesh unto my skin.
Dor. Truly, Master Strumbo, you speak too learnedly for
    me to understand the drift of your mind, and there-
    fore tell your tale in plain terms, and leave off   85
    your dark riddles.
Strum. Alas, Mistress Dorothy, this is my luck, that
    when I most would, I cannot be understood, so that
    my great learning is an inconvenience unto me. But
    to speak in plain terms, I love you, Mistress   90
    Dorothy, if you like to accept me into your
    familiarity.
Dor. If this be all, I am content.
Strum. Sayest thou so, sweet wench? Let me lick thy

83. Master] *Simms*; M. *Q*.

---

  68. *letters*] epistle; the plural has a singular meaning in a
formal sense, and Dorothy may be poking fun at Strumbo by referring
to his letter as a formal piece of writing.
  72. *pigsney*] "an endearing form of address...Chiefly applied to a
girl or woman" (*O.E.D.*, arch. and *dial.*, 1.a).
  73. *ingeny*] ingenuity.
  77-82.] doggerel rhyming typical of the Elizabethan clown; cf. the
Friar, Novice, and Guenthian in *Edward I*, ii, 313ff.

62   TRAGEDY OF LOCRINE   [ACT I

    toes. Farewell, Mistress. *Turning to the*   95
    people. If any of you be in love, provide ye a
    capcase full of new coined words, and then shall
    you soon have the succado de labres, and something
    else.   *Exeunt.*

SCENE IV

Enter LOCRINE, GUENDOLINE, CAMBER, ALBANACT, CORINEUS,
          ASSARACUS, DEBON, THRASIMACHUS.

Loc. Uncle, and princes of brave Brittany,
   Since that our noble father is entombed,
   As best beseemed so brave a prince as he,
   If so you please, this day my love and I,
   Within the temple of Concordia,   5
   Will solemnize our royal marriage.
Thra. Right noble lord, your subjects every one
   Must needs obey your highness at command,
   Especially in such a cause as this,
   That much concerns your highness' great content.   10
Loc. Then frolic, lordings, to fair Concord's walls,
   Where we will pass the day in knightly sports,
   The night in dancing and in figured masks,
   And offer to god Risus all our sports.   *Exeunt.*

95-96. *Turning to the people.*] *Simms*; after 93 *Q.*

---

   97. *capcase*] "receptacle of any kind" (*O.E.D.*, *Obs.*, 2).
   98. *succado de labres*] kiss, here a corruption of "sweetness of
the lips."

I.iv.1. *Brittany*] Britain.
2. *that*] used as a conjunctional affix (Abbott, sec. 287).
13. *figured*] i.e., symbolic masks.
14. *Risus*] god of laughter.

ACT II

SCENE I

Enter ATE *as before. After a little lightning and thundering, let there come forth this show:* PERSEUS *and* ANDROMEDA, *hand in hand, and* CEPHEUS *also with swords and targets. Then let there come out of another door,* PHINEUS, *all black in armour, with* Ethiopians *after him, driving in* PERSEUS, *and having taken away* ANDROMEDA, *let them depart.* ATE *remaining, saying:*

Ate. Regit omnia numen.
When Perseus married fair Andromeda,
The only daughter of King Cepheus,
He thought he had established well his crown,
And that his kingdom should for aye endure.   5
But, lo, proud Phineus with a band of men,
Contrived of sunburnt Ethiopians,
By force of arms the bride he took from him,

0.1. ATE] Hazlitt; Atey *Q*; Ate Rowe.

0.4. *targets*] light, round shields.
1.] "Fate rules all things" (Moltke).
2-9.] Cepheus, in order to save his kingdom, was forced to offer Andromeda as a sacrifice to a dragon, but Perseus slew the dragon and was rewarded with Andromeda's hand in marriage. The brother of Cepheus, Phineus, had been engaged to Andromeda, and he broke up the wedding feast; in the Ovidian story, however, Perseus saved his bride by raising the Gorgon's head and turning his attackers to stone, including Phineus (see Ovid, *Metamorphoses*, IV, V).
7. *Contrived of*] made up of; not recorded in the *O.E.D.*

    And turned their joy into a flood of tears.
    So fares it with young Locrine and his love.   10
    He thinks this marriage tendeth to his weal,
    But this foul day, this foul accursèd day,
    Is the beginning of his miseries.
    Behold where Humber and his Scythians
    Approacheth nigh with all his warlike train.   15
    I need not, I, the sequel shall declare,
    What tragic chances fall out in this war.   [*Exit.*]

SCENE II

Enter HUMBER, HUBBA, ESTRILD, SEGAR *and their soldiers.*

Hum. At length the snail doth climb the highest tops,
    Ascending up the stately castle walls;
    At length the water with continual drops,
    Doth penetrate the hardest marble stone;
    At length we are arrived in Albion.   5
    Nor could the barbarous Dacian sovereign,
    Nor yet the ruler of brave Belgia
    Stay us from cutting over to this isle;
    Whereas I hear a troop of Phrygians
    Under the conduct of Posthumius' son,   10

17. *Exit.*] Rowe.
II.ii.0.1. ESTRILD] *Rowe*; Estrilo *Q*.   10. Posthumius'] *F*; Postumius *Q*.

---

    14. *Scythians*] Scythia is the region north of the Black Sea, and the "people of this countrey are descriued to be cruell, sauage, and wilde" (Cooper); in the source material, only Holinshed, Fabyan and Lodge call the invaders Scythians (Erbe, "Die Locrinesage," p. 67).
    II.ii.1-5.] Cf. *The Spanish Tragedy*, II,i,3-8; *Locrine* cited by Tilley, S581.
    6. *Dacian*] Dacia is the region north of Thrace.
    8. *cutting*] crossing.
    9. *Phrygians*] Trojans; Phrygia comprised "part of the central plateau and the western flank of Asia Minor" (*O.C.D.*).
    10. *Posthumius*] "The son of Aeneas, by Lauinia, called also Syluius" (Cooper).

SC. II]   TRAGEDY OF LOCRINE   65

   Have pitchèd up lordly pavilions,
   And hope to prosper in this lovely isle.
   But I will frustrate all their foolish hope,
   And teach them that the Scythian emperor
   Leads Fortune tièd in a chain of gold,   15
   Constaining her to yield unto his will
   And grace him with their regal diadem,
   Which I will have maugre their treble hosts,
   And all the power their petty kings can make.
Hub. If she that rules fair Rhamnus' golden gate   20
   Grant us the honour of the victory,
   As hitherto she always favoured us,
   Right noble father, we will rule the land,
   Enthronizèd in seats of topaz stones,
   That Locrine and his brethren all may know   25
   None must be king but Humber and his son.
Hum. Courage, my son; Fortune shall favour us,
   And yield to us the coronet of bay
   That decketh none but noble conquerors.
   But what saith Estrild to these regions?   30
   How liketh she the temperature thereof?
   Are they not pleasant in her gracious eyes?
Est. The plains, my lord, garnished with Flora's wealth
   And overspread with parti-coloured flowers,
   Do yield sweet contentation to my mind;   35

20. Rhamnus'] *Hazlitt*; Rhamnis *Q*.   33. Est.] *Rowe*; Astr. *Q*.

15-16.] Cf. *Alphonsus*, IV,iii,1481-82: "I clap vp *Fortune* in a cage of gold,/ To make her turne her wheele as I thinke best"; both plays were probably influenced by *Tamburlaine, Part I*, I,ii,173-74: "I hold the Fates bound fast in iron chains,/ And with my hand turn Fortune's wheel about." The same idea occurs in *Selimus*, 1.2411.
 18. *maugre*] in spite of.
 20. *Rhamnus*] a sanctuary in Attica, containing a temple to Nemesis (*O.C.D.*); cf. *Selimus*, 11.676-77: "...thou blindfull mistresse of mishap,/ Chiefe pratronesse of *Rhamus* golden gates."
 28. *coronet*] "garland" (Onions).
 31. *temperature*] has the obsolete meaning of a "temperate condition of the weather or climate" (*O.E.D.*, 6).
 33. *Flora*] goddess of flowers.
 35. *contentation*] contentment or satisfaction (*O.E.D.*, 3, arch.).

         The airy hills enclosed with shady groves,
         The groves replenished with sweet chirping birds,
         The birds resounding heavenly melody,
         Are equal to the groves of Thessaly,
         Where Phoebus with the learned ladies nine   40
         Delight themselves with music's harmony;
         And from the moisture of the mountain tops
         The silent springs dance down with murmuring streams,
         And water all the ground with crystal waves;
         The gentle blasts of Eurus' modest wind,   45
         Moving the pittering leaves of Sylvan's woods,
         Do equal it with Tempe's paradise;
         And thus consorted all to one effect,
         Do make me think these are the happy isles,
         Most fortunate, if Humber may them win.   50
Hub.   Madam, where resolution leads the way
         And courage follows with emboldened pace,
         Fortune can never use her tyranny;
         For valiantness is like unto a rock
         That standeth in the waves of ocean,   55
         Which though the billows beat on every side,

41. music's] *Simms*; musicke *Q*; musicke's *Rowe*. 48. consorted] *Rowe*; comforted *Q*.

   36-38.] the "marching figure" where a key word of one line becomes the subject of the next (Puttenham, *English Poesie*, Bk. III, chap. xix).
   39. *Thessaly*] "district of northern Greece" (*O.C.D.*).
   40.] Phoebus, the god of music and poetry, and the nine muses.
   45. *Eurus*] the east wind (Cooper).
   46. *pittering*] "the sound made by the grasshopper, or by a thin stream of water running over stones"; cf. *Selimus*, 1.501: "And when his pittering streames are low & thin" (*O.E.D.*).
   46. *Sylvan*] Sylvanus, the god of woods.
   47. *Tempe*] "A place in Thessalia wonderfull pleasant, hauynge trees and medowes meruaylous delectable, wherein byrdes of diuers kyndes do singe continually with excellent melodie: thereof all pleasant wooddes haue the name of *Tempe*" (Cooper).
   49-50. *happy...fortunate*] the blessed or fortunate islands, "the mythical winterless home of the happy dead, far west on Ocean shores or islands" (*O.C.D.*).
   55. *ocean*] trisyllabic here.

SC. II]   TRAGEDY OF LOCRINE   67

    And Boreas fell, with his tempestuous storms,
    Bloweth upon it with a hideous clamour,
    Yet it remaineth still unmoveable.
Hum. Kingly resolved, thou glory of thy sire.   60
    But, worthy Segar, what uncouth novelties
    Bringst thou unto our royal majesty?
Seg. My lord, the youngest of all Brutus' sons,
    Stout Albanact, with millions of men,
    Approacheth nigh, and meaneth ere the morn 65
    To try your force by dint of fatal sword.
Hum. Tut, let him come with millions of hosts;
    He shall find entertainment good enough,
    Yea, fit for those that are our enemies:
    For we'll receive them at the lances' points, 70
    And massacre their bodies with our blades.
    Yea, though they were in number infinite,
    More than the mighty Babylonian queen,
    Semiramis, the ruler of the West,
    Brought 'gainst the emperor of the Scythians, 75
    Yet would we not start back one foot from them,
    That they might know we are invincible.
Hub. Now, by great Jove, the supreme king of heaven,
    And the immortal gods that live therein,
    Whenas the morning shows his cheerful face 80
    And Lucifer, mounted upon his steed,
    Brings in the chariot of the golden sun,

57. Boreas] *F*; Borras *Q*.

---

 57. *Boreas*] north wind.
 61. *uncouth novelties*] strange new matters; *Locrine* cited in the *O.E.D.* (Novelty, 1.b, *Obs*.).
 64. *millions*] countless.
 66. *by...sword*] "by dint of sword" is an obsolete phrase meaning "by force of arms" (*O.E.D.*, Dint, *sb*., 2.b).
 68. *entertainment*] manner of reception.
 74. *Semiramis*] ruled Assyria for many years and was famous in war (*O.C.D.*).
 80. *as*] conjunctional suffix (Abbott, sec. 116).
 81. *Lucifer*] the morning star.

I'll meet young Albanact in the open field,
And crack my lance upon his burgonet
To try the valour of his boyish strength.   85
There will I show such ruthful spectacles,
And cause so great effusion of blood
That all his boys shall wonder at my strength;
As when the warlike queen of Amazon,
Penthesilea, armèd with her lance,   90
Girt with a corslet of bright shining steel,
Cooped up the faint-heart Grecians in the camp.

Hum. Spoke like a warlike knight, my noble son;
Nay, like a prince that seeks his father's joy.
Therefore, tomorrow, ere fair Titan shine,   95
And bashful Eos, messenger of light,
Expels the liquid sleep from out men's eyes,
Thou shalt conduct the right wing of the host;
The left wing shall be under Segar's charge;
The rearward shall be under me myself.   100
And, lovely Estrild, fair and gracious,
If Fortune favour me in mine attempts,
Thou shalt be queen of lovely Albion.
Fortune shall favour me in mine attempts,
And make thee queen of lovely Albion.   105
Come, let us in, and muster up our train
And furnish up our lusty soldiers
That they may be a bulwark to our state,
And bring our wishèd joys to perfect end. [*Exeunt.*]

109. *Exeunt.*] F.

---

84. *burgonet*] "light casque or steel cap" (Onions).
89-92.] Penthesilea, proficient in battle, fought on the Trojan side after Hector's death; she was killed by Achilles (*O.C.D.*).
95. *Titan*] the sun god.
96. *Eos*] goddes of dawn, often called Aurora.
97. *liquid sleep*] The phrase is employed by Valerius Flaccus in the *Argonautica*, IV,16, "*quem penes alta quies liquidique potentia somni*" (noted by Dr. R.E. Fantham, Trinity College, University of Toronto).
107. *furnish up*] "To fit up with proper equipment" (*O.E.D.*, Furnish, *v.*, 10.c.(b), *Obs.*).

SC III] TRAGEDY OF LOCRINE 69

SCENE III

Enter STRUMBO, DOROTHY, TROMPART *cobbling shoes and singing.*

Trom. We cobblers lead a merry life,
All. Dan, dan, dan, dan,
Strum. Void of all envy and of strife,
All. Dan diddle dan.
Dor. Our ease is great, our labour small, 5
All. Dan, dan, dan, dan,
Strum. And yet our gains be much withal,
All. Dan diddle dan.
Dor. With this art so fine and fair,
All. Dan, dan, dan, dan 10
Trom. No occupation may compare,
All. Dan diddle dan.
Strum. For merry pastime and joyful glee,
All. Dan, dan, dan, dan,
Dor. Most happy men we cobblers be, 15
All. Dan diddle dan.
Trom. The can stands full of nappy ale,
All. Dan, dan, dan, dan,
Strum. In our shop still withouten fail,
All. Dan diddle dan. 20

SCENE III] *Rowe;* The 2. Scene *Q;* Scena Tertia *F.* 3. envy] *F;* ennie *Q.*

1-36.] drinking song; cf. Barnabie Bunch in *The Weakest Goeth to the Wall,* sig. B2-B2^V (John Robert Moore, "The Songs of the Public Theatres in the Time of Shakespeare," (*Journal of English and Germanic Philology,* 28 (1929), 180, 189). Strumbo's song, "We cobblers lead a merry life," has been set for men's voices (TTBB, unaccompanied) by Felix White (J. Curwen & Sons Ltd., 1933).
  17. *can*] "vessel for holding liquids," formerly included drinking vessels (*O.E.D., sb.*^{1}, 1).
  17. *nappy*] strong.
  19. *withouten*] archaic form retained for rhythm.

Dor. This is our meat, this is our food,
All. Dan, dan, dan, dan,
Trom. This brings us to a merry mood,
All. Dan diddle dan.
Strum. This makes us work for company,[*Enter* Captain.]25
All. Dan, dan, dan, dan,
Dor. To pull the tankards cheerfully,
All. Dan diddle dan.
Trom. Drink to thy husband, Dorothy,
All. Dan, dan, dan, dan, 30
Dor. Why then, my Strumbo, there's to thee,
All. Dan diddle dan.
Strum. Drink thou the rest, Trompart, amain,
All. Dan, dan, dan, dan,
Dor. When that is gone we'll fill't again, 35
All. Dan diddle dan.
Cap. [*Aside*] The poorest state is farthest from annoy;
 How merrily he sitteth on his stool.
 But when he sees that needs he must be pressed,
 He'll turn his note and sing another tune. 40
 [*Coming forward.*]
 Ho, by your leave, master cobbler.
Strum. You are welcome, gentleman. What, will you any
 old shoes or buskins, or will you have your shoes

25. *Enter* Captain.] *This ed.* 37. *Aside*] *This ed.* 40.1. *Coming forward.*] *This ed.*

---

 25. *for company*] i.e., for company's sake.
 27. *pull*] drink liquor from; *Locrine* cited in the *O.E.D.* (v., 12).
 33. *amain*] without delay.
 37. *state*] condition with regard to property or riches.
 37. *annoy*] vexation or trouble.
 39. *pressed*] forced to serve in the army; the number of men conscripted in the years 1594-1599 ranged from 1,806 in 1595 to 9,164 in 1598 (Paul A. Jorgensen, *Shakespeare's Military World* (Berkeley: University of California Press, 1956), p. 130).
 40. *turn...note*] change his way of thinking (*O.E.D.*, Note, $sb.^2$, 5.b).
 43. *buskins*] "half-boots" (Onions).

SC. III]   TRAGEDY OF LOCRINE   71

    clouted? I will do them as well as any cobbler in
    Caithness whatsoever.   45
Cap. O, master cobbler, you are far deceived in me, for
    don't you see this? *Showing him press-money.* I
    come not to buy any shoes, but to buy yourself;
    come, Sir, you must be a soldier in the king's
    cause.   50
Strum. Why, but hear you, Sir, has your king any com-
    mission to take any man against his will? I promise
    you, I can scant believe it. Or did he give you
    commission?
Cap. O, Sir, ye need not care for that. I need no   55
    commission. Hold here; I command you, in the name
    of our king Albanact, to appear tomorrow in the
    town-house of Caithness.
Strum. King Nactaball, I cry God mercy! what have we to
    do with him, or he with us? But you, Sir, Master   60
    Capontail, draw your pasteboard, or else I promise
    you, I'll give you a canvasado with a bastinado over

45. Caithness] *Hazlitt*; Cathues *Q*; Cathness *M*. 47. don't] *Hazlitt*;
don *Q*. 47. *Showing him press-money.*] *Hazlitt*; after 45 *Q*. 58.
Caithness] *Hazlitt*; Cathnes *Q*; Cathness *M*. 59. Nactaball] *Rowe*;
Nactabell *Q*. 61. Capontail] *Simms*; capoutaile *Q*; capontail *F*.
62. bastinado] *F*; basti-nano *Q*.

---

    44. *cloutod*] "patched" (Onions).
    45. *Caithness*] name used in the *Historia* for the land beyond the Humber (Tatlock, *Legendary History*, p. 10).
    47. *press-money*] "paid to a sailor or soldier on his enlistment, the acceptance of which was the legal proof of his engagement" (*O.E.D.*, 3).
    58. *town-house*] "A municipal building containing the public offices, court-house, and Town Hall" (*O.E.D.*, 1).
    59. *Nactaball*] comic perversion of Albanact.
    61. *Capontail*] perhaps has the meaining of "coward," from the French word "*capon*."
    61. *pasteboard*] a stiff material made by pasting and compressing three or more sheets of paper; perhaps the roll in which the Captain enters names of those to be pressed. In this sense, "draw" in the phrase "draw your pasteboard" has the meaning "withdraw" (Onions).
    62. *canvasado*] a thrashing.
    62. *bastinado*] "beating with a stick"; cf. *AYL*, V,i,61: "I will deal in poison with thee, or in bastinado, or in steel" (Onions).

your shoulders, and teach you to come hither with your implements.

Cap. I pray thee, good fellow, be content; I do the king's command. 65

Strum. Put me out of your book then.

Cap. I may not.

Strum. Snatching up a staff. No will? Come, Sir, will your stomach serve you? By gog's blue hood and halidom, I will have a bout with you. *Fight both.* 70

Enter THRASIMACHUS.

Thra. How now, what noise, what sudden clamour's this? How now, my captain and the cobbler so hard at it? Sirs, what is your quarrel?

Cap. Nothing, Sir, but that he will not take press- money. 75

Thra. Here, good fellow, take it at my command, unless you mean to be stretched.

Strum. Truly, master gentleman, I lack no money; if you please, I will resign it to one of these poor fellows. 80

Thra. No such matter. Look you be at the common-house tomorrow. *Exit* THRASIMACHUS *and the* Captain.

71. a bout] *M*; about *Q*. 77-78.] *Simms*; verse *Q*.

---

64. *implements*] instruments (in legal sense).
69. *No will?*] i.e., are you unwilling?
69-70. *will...you*] do you have enough courage.
70. *gog's*] perversion of god's; cf. *Shr.*, III,ii,163: "by gogs-wouns" (Onions).
70. *blue hood*] probably a reference to a blue-cap or a Scotchman (Onions); Strumbo later enters (IV,iii,20.1) wearing a Scotch cap.
71. *halidom*] "originally the holy relics upon which oaths were sworn, the ancient formula being 'as helpe me God and halidome', altered later to 'by my halidome', which was subsequently used by itself as a weak asseveration"; cf. *Gent.*, IV,ii,138: "By my halidome, I was fast asleep" (Onions).
78. *stretched*] hanged.
82. *common-house*] recognized by the law as an establishment bound to serve the public; see n. 1.58.

SC. III] TRAGEDY OF LOCRINE 73

Strum. O, wife, I have spun a fair thread; if I had been
 quiet, I had not been pressed, and therefore well 85
 may I wayment. But come, sirrah, shut up, for we
 must to the wars. *Exeunt.*

SCENE IV

Enter ALBANACT, DEBON, THRASIMACHUS, *and the* Lords.

Alb. Brave cavaliers, princes of Albany,
 Whose trenchant blades with our deceasèd sire,
 Passing the frontiers of brave Grecia,
 Were bathèd in our enemies' lukewarm blood,
 Now is the time to manifest your wills, 5
 Your haughty minds and resolutions;
 Now opportunity is offerèd
 To try your courage and your earnest zeal,
 Which you always protest to Albanact;
 For at this time, yea at this present time, 10
 Stout fugitives, come from the Scythians' bounds,
 Have pestered every place with mutinies.
 But trust me, lordings, I will never cease
 To persecute the rascal runagates,
 Till all the rivers stainèd with their blood 15
 Shall fully show their fatal overthrow.
Deb. So shall your highness merit great renown,
 And imitate your agèd father's steps.

86. sirrah] *Simms*; sirrha *Q*.

---

84. *I...thread*] proverbial--to be your own worst enemy (Tilley, T252, "You have spun a fine (fair) Thread.").
 86. *wayment*] lament; *Locrine* cited in *O.E.D.* (v. *Obs.*, 1, *intr.*).
 II.iv.1. *cavaliers*] from "cavaleiro," a "gentleman trained in arms...(hence) gallant" (Onions).
 2. *trenchant*] "cutting, sharp" (Onions).
 14. *runagates*] "vagabonds" (Onions).

Alb. But tell me, cousin, cam'st thou through the plains?
And saw'st thou there the faint-heart fugitives 20
Mustering their weather-beaten soldiers?
What order keep they in their marshalling?
Thra. After we passed the groves of Caledon,
Where murmuring rivers slide with silent streams,
We did behold the straggling Scythians' camp, 25
Replete with men, stored with munition;
There might we see the valiant-minded knights
Fetching careers along the spacious plains.
Humber and Hubba, armed in azure blue,
Mounted upon their coursers white as snow, 30
Went to behold the pleasant flowering fields;
Hector and Troilus, Priamus' lovely sons,
Chasing the Grecians over Simois,
Were not to be compared to these two knights.
Alb. Well hast thou painted out in eloquence 35
The protraiture of Humber and his son,
As fortunate as was Polycrates;
Yet should they not escape our conquering swords,
Or boast of aught but of our clemency.

Enter STRUMBO *and* TROMPART, *crying often.*

Both. Wildfire and pitch, wildfire and pitch, &c. 40
Thra. What, Sirs, what mean you by these clamours made,
These outcries raised in our stately court?

28. careers] *Simms;* carriers *Q;* carreers *Rowe.* 32. Troilus] *F;* Troialus *Q.* 33. Simois] *Hazlitt;* Simoeis *Q.* 42. These] *M;* Those *Q.*

---

23. *Caledon*] in the *Historia*, refers vaguely to the "wilds of Scotland" (Tatlock, *Legendary History*, p. 16).
28. *Fetching*] making.
28. *careers*] short gallops at full speed (Onions).
30. *courser*] "large powerful horse, ridden in battle" (*O.E.D.*, sb.^{2}, 1).
33. *Simois*] a river at Troy.
37. *Polycrates*] a tyrant of Samos who never suffered any misfortune; he decided to satisfy fortune by throwing a valuable ring into the sea, but the ring was returned to him in a fish.
41-42.] Cf. *Looking-Glasse*, III,ii,1153: "How now? what meane these outcries in our Court?"

SC. IV] TRAGEDY OF LOCRINE   75

Strum. Wildfire and pitch, wildfire and pitch.
Thra. Villains, I say, tell us the cause hereof.
Strum. Wildfire and pitch, &c.   45
Thra. Tell me, you villains, why you make this noise,
   Or with my lance I will prick your bowels out.
Alb. Where are your houses? where's your dwelling place?
Strum. Place? Ha, ha, ha! laugh a month and a day at
   him. Place! I cry God mercy, why do you think   50
   that such poor honest men as we be, hold our
   habitacles in kings' palaces? Ha, ha, ha! But
   because you seem to be an abominable chieftain, I
   will tell you our state:
  From the top to the toe,   55
  From the head to the shoe;
  From the beginning to the ending,
  From the building to the burning.
   This honest fellow and I had our mansion-cottage in
   the suburbs of this city, hard by the temple of   60
   Mercury. Any by the common soldiers of the Shitens,
   the Scythians--what do you call them?--withal
   the suburbs were burnt to the ground, and the ashes
   are left there, for the country wives to wash bucks
   withal.   65
  And that which grieves me most,
  My loving wife,
  O cruel strife,

66-69.] *M*; prose *Q*.

---

 52. *habitacles*] habitations.
 53. *abominable*] probably Strumbo's perversion of "admirable."
 60-61. *suburbs...Mercury*] Strumbo may be alluding to the brothels as the London suburbs were known "as a place of inferior, debased and *esp.* licentious habits of life" (*O.E.D.*, 4.b, *Obs.*). Mercury was the patron god of thieves and cheating.
 64. *bucks*] a buck is the "quantity of clothes put through the 'buck' or lye" (Onions); see note I,iii,11. Ashes are used in the production of alkalized water or lye.

	The wicked flames did roast.	
	And therefore, Captain Crust,	70
	We will continually cry,	
	Except you seek a remedy	
	Our houses to re-edify	
	Which now are burnt to dust.	

Both. (*cry*) Wildfire and pitch, wildfire and pitch. 75
Alb. Well, we must remedy these outrages,
    And throw revenge upon their hateful heads.
    And you, good fellows, for your houses burnt,
    We will remunerate you store of gold,
    And build your houses by our palace gate. 80
Strum. Gate! O petty treason to my person! nowhere else
    but by your backside? Gate! O how I am vexed in
    my choler! Gate! I cry God mercy! Do you hear,
    master king? If you mean to gratify such poor men
    as we be, you must build our houses by the tavern. 85
Alb. It shall be done, Sir.
Strum. Near the tavern; ay, by our lady, Sir, it was
    spoken like a good fellow. Do you hear, Sir? When
    our house is builded, if you do chance to pass or
    repass that way, we will bestow a quart of the 90
    best wine upon you. *Exit.*
Alb. It grieves me, lordings, that my subjects' goods
    Should thus be spoilèd by the Scythians,
    Who, as you see, with lightfoot foragers
    Depopulate the places where they come. 95
    But, cursèd Humber, thou shalt rue the day,
    That e'er thou cam'st unto Caithnesia. *Exeunt.*

73. re-edify] *F2*; redifie *Q*.   87. by our lady] *M*; by ladie *Q*.
97. Caithnesia] *This ed.*; Cathuesia *Q*; Cathnesia *F*.

---

    70. *Captain*] a familiar "term of address (without implying any office or rank)" (*O.E.D.*, *sb.*, 12).
    81. *petty treason*] "treason against a subject" (*O.E.D.*, Treason, *sb.*, 2.b).
    82. *backside*] i.e., near the palace gate.
    87. *by...lady*] common oath; Malone's emendation appears correct.
    94. *foragers*] ravagers.

SCENE V

Enter HUMBER, HUBBA, SEGAR, TRUSSIER, *and their soldiers.*

Hum. Hubba, go take a coronet of our horse,
    As many lancers and light-armèd knights
    As may suffice for such an enterprise,
    And place them in the grove of Caledon.
    With these, when as the skirmish doth increase,   5
    Retire thou from the shelters of the wood,
    And set upon the weakened Trojans' backs;
    For policy joinèd with chivalry
    Can never be put back from victory.   *Exit* [HUBBA.]
        ALBANACT *enter and say, clowns with him,*
Alb. Thou base-born Hun, how durst thou be so sold   10
    As once to menace warlike Albanact,
    The great commander of these regions?
    But thou shalt buy thy rashness with thy death,
    And rue too late thy over-bold attempts;
    For with this sword, this instrument of death,   15
    That hath been drenchèd in my foeman's blood,
    I'll separate thy body from thy head,
    And set that coward blood of thine abroach.
Strum. Nay, with this staff, great Strumbo's instrument,
    I'll crack thy cockscomb, paltry Scythian.   20

2. lancers] *Simms*; launciers *Q*; lanciers *Rowe*.   9. HUBBA] *McKerrow*.

   0.1 TRUSSIER] does not have a speaking part; enters again at II,
vii where he is referred to in the 1595 quarto as "Thrassier."
   1. *coronet*] a cornet, "company of cavalry, so called from its
standard, which was originally a long horn-shaped pennon" (Onions);
cf. *The Battle of Alcazar*, I,ii,189: "take a cornet of our horse."
   6. *Retire*] come back.
   8. *policy*] synonymous with trickery by the mid-16th century (Mario
Praz, "Machiavelli and the Elizabethans," *Proceedings of the British
Academy*, 14 (1928), 59).
   18. set...abroach] i.e., to pierce the body and let the blood run
forth.
   20. *cockscomb*] fool's cap "like a cock's comb in shape and colour"
(Onions); here the term is used for "head."

78   TRAGEDY OF LOCRINE   [ACT II

Hum. Nor reck I of thy threats, thou princox boy;
    Nor do I fear thy foolish insolence.
    And but thou better use thy bragging blade
    Than thou dost rule thy overflowing tongue,
    Superbious Briton, thou shalt know too soon   25
    The force of Humber and his Scythians.
Let them fight. HUMBER *and his soldiers run in.* [ALBAN-
            ACT *and his forces follow.*]
Strum. O horrible, terrible!   [*Exit.*]

SCENE VI

Sound the alarm. Enter HUMBER *and his soldiers.*

Hum. How bravely this young Briton, Albanact,
    Darteth abroad the thunderbolts of war,
    Beating down millions with his furious mood,
    And in his glory triumphs over all;
    Moving the massy squadrants of the ground,   5
    Heap hills on hills, to scale the starry sky,
    As when Briareus, armed with an hundred hands,
    Flung forth an hundred mountains at great Jove,
    And when the monstrous giant, Monichus,

22. insolence] *Simms*; insolencie *Q*.   26.1-.2. ALBANACT *and his forces follow.*] Hazlitt.   27. *Exit.*] *Simms*.
SCENE VI] *Simms*; The sixt Act. *Q*.   7. As when] *F*; When *Q*.

---

21. *princox*] "pert saucy boy" (Onions).
23. *but*] except; "unless" is now used in this sense (Abbott, sec. 120).
23-24.] Cf. *Selimus*, 11.2457-58: "But thou canst better vse thy bragging blade,/ Then thou canst rule thy ouerflowing tongue."
25. *Superbious*] proud, insolent.
II,vi,1-18.] See Introduction, p. 8 and Appendix C.
3. *mood*] courage.
5. *squadrants*] square pieces; *Locrine* cited in the *O.E.D.* (*sb.*, 1, *obs.*)
7. *As when*] The Folio emendation introduces the comparison and completes the parallelism with 1.9.
7. *Briareus*] hundred-handed giant of Greek mythology.
9. *Monichus*] "one of the Centaures" (Cooper).

SC. VI]   TRAGEDY OF LOCRINE   79

    Hurled Mount Olympus at great Mars his targe,   10
    And shot huge cedars at Minerva's shield.
    How doth he overlook with haughty front
    My fleeting hosts, and lifts his lofty face
    Against us all that now do fear his force;
    Like as we see the wrathful sea from far,   15
    In a great mountain heaped, with hideous noise,
    With thousand billows beat against the ships,
    And toss them in the waves like tennis balls.
                                 Sound the alarm.
    Ay me! I fear my Hubba is surprised.
    Sound again. Enter ALBANACT [*and soldiers.*]
Alb. Follow me, soldiers, follow Albanact;   20
    Pursue the Scythians flying through the field.
    Let none of them escape with victory,
    That they may know the Britons' force is more
    Than all the power of the trembling Huns.
Thra. Forward, brave soldiers, forward; keep the chase. 25
    He that takes captive Humber or his son,
    Shall be rewarded with a crown of gold.
Sound alarm; then let them fight. HUMBER *give back.*
HUBBA *enter at their backs, and kill* DEBON; *let* STRUMBO
fall down. ALBANACT *run in, and afterwards enter wounded.*
Alb. Injurious Fortune, hast thou crossed me thus?
    Thus in the morning of my victories,

19. om. *Hum.*] *Rowe;* Humb. *Q.*   19.1. *and soldiers.*] *Moltke.*

---

  10. *Mars his*] "His" sometimes indicated the possessive "'s," especially following a proper name and more frequently when the name ended in "s"; cf. *1H6*, I,ii,1: "Mars his true moving" (Abbott, sec. 217).
  11. *Minerva*] Roman goddess of wisdom.
  12. *front*] forehead or face.
  18. *tennis balls*] idea of fortune embodied in a game of tennis (Grover Smith, "The Tennis-Ball of Fortune," *Notes & Queries*, ser. 16, 190 (1946), 202-203).
  27. *crown*] coin (*O.E.D.*, sb., 8.a and b).
  27.2. *enter...backs*] ambush; required, also, in the staging of *Alphonsus*.

Thus in the prime of my felicity 30
To cut me off by such hard overthrow;
Hadst thou no time thy rancour to declare,
But in the spring of all my dignities?
Hadst thou no place to spit thy venom out
But on the person of young Albanact? 35
I, that erewhile did scare mine enemies
And drove them almost to a shameful flight;
I, that erewhile full lion-like did fare
Amongst the dangers of the thick-thronged pikes,
Must now depart, most lamentably slain 40
By Humber's treacheries and Fortune's spites.
Cursed be her charms, damned be her cursèd charms,
That doth delude the wayward hearts of men,
Of men that trust unto her fickle wheel,
Which never leaveth turning upside down. 45
O gods, O heavens, allot me but the place
Where I may find her hateful mansion,
I'll pass the Alps to wat'ry Meroe,
Where fiery Phoebus in his chariot,
The wheels whereof are decked with emeralds, 50
Casts such a heat, yea such a scorching heat,
And spoileth Flora of her chequered grass;
I'll overrun the mountain Caucasus,

42. her charms] *Rowe*; their charms *Q*. 49. Phoebus] *F*; Fhoebus *Q*.
51. Casts] *Rowe*; Cast *Q*. 53. Caucasus] *F*; Cancusus *Q*.

---

42. *her charms*] Both Rowe and McKerrow suggest reading "her" for the quarto "their," and this seems necessary in view of the dramatist's fondness for writing parallel phrases with only minor modulation.
44-45.] the medieval idea of tragedy--Fortune turning her wheel.
48. *Meroe*] an island in the river Nile.
48.] Cf. *Orlando Furioso* (printed quarto), 1.1182: "Tell him Ile passe the Alpes, and vp to Meroe"; *Locrine* has also been influenced by the corresponding line in the Alleyn MS., 11.249-250: "Ile vp the Alpes, and post to Meroe the/ watry lakishe hill." W.W. Greg (*Two Elizabethan Stage Abridgements: The Battle of Alcazar & Orlando Furioso* (Oxford: Oxford University Press, for the Malone Society, 1922), p. 234) discusses the relationship between *Orlando* and *Locrine* and the bearing this relationship has on the dating of both works.

SC. VI]   TRAGEDY OF LOCRINE   81

    Where fell Chimaera in her triple shape
    Rolleth hot flames from out her monstrous paunch,   55
    Scaring the beasts with issue of her gorge;
    I'll pass the frozen zone, where icy flakes,
    Stopping the passage of the fleeting ships,
    Do lie like mountains in the congealed sea;
    Where if I find that hateful house of hers,   60
    I'll pull the fickle wheel from out her hands,
    And tie herself in everlasting bands.
    But all in vain I breathe these threatenings;
    The day is lost, the Huns are conquerors,
    Debon is slain, my men are done to death,   65
    The currents swift swim violently with blood;
    And last, O that this last night so long last,
    Myself with wounds past all recovery,
    Must leave my crown for Humber to possess.
Strum. Lord have mercy upon us. Masters, I think this 70
    is a holiday; every man lies sleeping in the fields,
    but, God knows, full sore against their wills.
Thra. Fly, noble Albanact, and save thyself.
    The Scythians follow with great celerity,
    And there's no way but flight, or speedy death;   75
    Fly, noble Albanact, and save thyself.   [*Exit.*]
                                Sound the alarm.
Alb. Nay, let them fly that fear to die the death,
    That tremble at the name of fatal Mors.

75. flight] *Rowe*; fight *Q*.   76. Exit.] *Moltke*.

---

54. *Chimaera*] "a monster hauing three heades, one like a lyon, an other like a goat, the thirde like a dragon" (Cooper).
57. *icy flakes*] ice bergs.
61.] Cf. Alleyn MS., ll.250-51: "and pull the harpe/ from out the ministrills h⟨a d⟩es"; Albanact's threat, that he will destroy Fortune's power, is similar to Orlando's challenge to Apollo in both the quarto and the Alleyn MS. See Baldwin, *Literary Genetics*, pp. 215-17; Baldwin cites Bernhardi (*Greene's Leben* (1874), p. 34) for pointing out the parallels between *Orlando* and *Locrine*.
67.] i.e., finally, may this night last a long time because it is the last night.

Ne'er shall proud Humber boast or brag himself
That he hath put young Albanact to flight; 80
And lest he should triumph at my decay,
This sword shall reave his master of his life,
That oft hath saved his master's doubtful life.
But O, my brethren, if you care for me,
Revenge my death upon his traitorous head. 85
Et vos queis domus est nigrantis regia Ditis,
Qui regitis rigido Stygios moderamine lucos:
Nox caeci regina poli, furialis Erinnys
Diique deaeque omnes, Albanum tollite regem,
Tollite flumineis undis rigidaque palude! 90
Nunc me fata vocant, hoc condam pectore ferrum.
                                    Thrust himself through.
                    Enter TROMPART.
Trom. O, what hath he done? His nose bleeds. But, O,
  I smell a fox; look where my master lies. Master,
  master!
Strum. Let me alone, I tell thee, for I am dead. 95
Trom. Yet one word, good master.

86. est] *F*; ect *Q*.   96. word] *M*; good *Q*.

---

82. *reave*] to take by violence (*O.E.D.*, $v.^1$, 4, *Obs.*).
83.] i.e., has often saved his life when it was in doubt.
86-91.] And you who sway in Pluto's royal house,
   And govern with stern power the Stygian realms,
   Night, queen of cloudy heavens--thou fearful fury,
   And you, ye gods and goddesses, receive
   The Alban sovereign to your gloomy lake
   And ever-flowing streams!--The summoning fates
   Decree, and through this bosom goes the sword. (Moltke)
86-87.] Baldwin (*Literary Genetics*, p. 217) points out that these two lines appear to be a condensation of four lines from the quarto version of *Orlando*:
   O vos qui colttes lacusque laeosque profundos,
   Infernasque domus, & nigra palatia Ditis:
   Tuque Demogorgon qui noctis fata gubernas,
   Qui regis infernum,...   (11.1277-80)
93. *I...fox*] sounds proverbial; perhaps a variation on the proverb "I smell a Rat" (Tilley, R31), meaning to have suspicions.
95.] feigning death; cf. Falstaff, *1H4*, V,iv,111ff.
96. *word*] appears correct; quarto does not make sense.

SC. VI]   TRAGEDY OF LOCRINE   83

Strum. I will not speak, for I am dead, I tell thee.
Trom. And is my master dead?
    O sticks and stones, brickbats and bones,
    And is my master dead?   100
    O you cockatrices, and you bablatrices,
    That in the woods dwell;
    You briars and brambles, you cooks' shops and
        shambles,
    Come howl and yell.
    With howling and screaking, with wailing and weeping,
    Come you to lament.   105
    O colliers of Croydon, and rustics of Roydon,
    And fishers of Kent.
    For Strumbo the cobbler, the fine merry cobbler
    Of Caithness town: 110
    At this same stour, at this very hour
    Lies dead on the ground.
    O master, thieves, thieves, thieves!
Strum. Where be they? Cox me tunny, bobekin! let me be
    rising, be gone, we shall be robbed by-and-by.   115

                                                                Exeunt.

110. Caithness] *Hazlitt*; Cathnes *Q*; Cathness *M.*

    98-112.] Trompart uses the same rhetorical devices found in the serious lament; see Introduction, pp. 17-18.
    99. *brickbats*] pieces of brick.
    101. *cockatrices*] basilisks, fabulous reptiles "supposed to be hatched by a serpent from a cock's egg and said to kill by [their] breath and look" (Onions); the word may also refer to whores.
    101. *bablatrices*] sole occurrence appears to be in *Locrine*; *O.E.D.* suggests the meaning female babblers.
    103. *shambles*] meat-markets.
    105. *screaking*] "emission of a shrill cry" (*O.E.D., vbl. sb.*).
    107. *Croydon*] town near London.
    107. *Roydon*] name of two towns in Norfolk, one in Essex.
    111. *stour*] "Used by Spenser and his imitators for: Time of turmoil and stress... Used by Green, Lodge, and others, probably by misapprehension of Spenser, for: Occasion, place" (*O.E.D., sb.^{1}*, 3.a and b, *Obs.*). Both senses seem to apply here.
    113.] robbing corpses was common practice; cf. Dericke in *The Famous Victories*, 11.1883-85.
    114. *Cox me tunny*] exact meaning unknown; "Cox" is from "cock's," a corruption of "God's" (Onions), and "tunny" may refer to fish.
    114. *bobekin*] perhaps a variant of the oath "bodikin" meaning "God's dear body!" (*O.E.D.*, Bodikin, 2, *Obs.*).

SCENE VII

Enter HUMBER, HUBBA, SEGAR, TRUSSIER, ESTRILD, *and the soldiers.*

Hum. Thus from the dreadful shocks of furious Mars,
 Thundering alarms, and Rhamnusia's drum,
 We are retired with joyful victory.
 The slaughtered Trojans, squeltering in their blood,
 Infect the air with their carcasses, 5
 And are a prey for every ravenous bird.
Est. So perish they that are our enemies!
 So perish they that love not Humber's weal.
 And mighty Jove, commander of the world,
 Protect my love from all false treacheries. 10
Hum. Thanks, lovely Estrild, solace to my soul.
 But valiant Hubba, for thy chivalry
 Declared against the men of Albany,
 Lo, here a flow'ring garland wreathed of bay,
 As a reward for thy forward mind. 15
  Set it on his head.
Hub. This unexpected honour, noble sire,
 Will prick my courage unto braver deeds,
 And cause me to attempt such hard exploits,
 That all the world shall sound of Hubba's name.
Hum. And now, brave soldiers, for this good success, 20
 Carouse whole cups of Amazonian wine,
 Sweeter than nectar or ambrosia,
 And cast away the clods of cursèd care,

SCENE VII] *This ed.*; The 8. Act. *Q.* 0.1. TRUSSIER] *This ed.*; Thrassier *Q.*

---

 2. *Rhamnusia's*] Rhamnusia is another name for Nemesis.
 4. *squeltering*] obsolete variant of swelter, "to be bathed in liquid; hence, to welter, wallow"; *Locrine* cited in *O.E.D.* (Swelter, *v.*, 3, *Obs.*).
 5. *air*] bi-syllabic; see Abbott, sec. 485.
 21. *Carouse*] drink up or drain.
 22. *ambrosia*] in Greek mythology, the food of the gods.
 23. *clods*] pieces of earth; hence the heaviness of earthly cares.

SC. VII]   TRAGEDY OF LOCRINE   85

    With goblets crowned with Semeleius' gifts.
    Now let us march to Abis' silver streams   25
    That clearly glide along the champaign fields,
    And moist the grassy meads with humid drops.
    Sound drums and trumpets, sound up cheerfully,
    Sith we return with joy and victory.
                                                           [*Exeunt.*]

29. Exeunt.] Rowe.

---

    24. *Semeleius*] Semele was the mother of Bacchus.
    25. *Abis*] the Abi is the Humber river (Cooper); Spenser refers to it as the "aunciant *Abus*" (*Faerie Queene*, II,x,16).
    29. *Sith*] "seeing that"; often used between c.1520 and c.1670 "to express cause, while *since* was restricted to time" (*O.E.D.*, C.2, *conj.*).

ACT III

SCENE I

Enter ATE *as before. The dumb show:* a Crocodile *sitting on a river's bank, and a little* Snake *stinging it; then let both of them fall into the water.*

Ate. *Scelera in authorem cadunt.*
High on a bank by Nilus' boisterous streams,
Fearfully sat the Egyptian crocodile,
Dreadfully grinding in his sharp long teeth,
The broken bowels of a silly fish;   5
His back was armed against the dint of spear
With shields of brass that shined like burnished
   gold;
And as he strétched forth his cruel paws,

4. his] McKerrow; her Q.

0.2. *river's bank*] a property used to prevent the audience seeing the grave trap through which the crocodile and snake fall; cf. first dumb show in *The Weakest Goeth to the Wall* (William J. Lawrence, *Pre-Restoration Stage Studies* (Cambridge, Mass.: Harvard University Press, 1927), p. 159).
 1.] "The criminal must answer for his crime" (Moltke).
 4. *his*] The emendation is necessary in order that the pronoun agree with ll.6 and 8.
 5. *silly*] see note I,i,8.
 6-7.] Cf. "Visions of the worlds vanitie," ll.72-73: "Whose backe was arm'd against the dint of speare/ With shields of brasse, that shone like burnisht golde."

SC. I] TRAGEDY OF LOCRINE 87

  A subtle adder, creeping closely near,
  Thrusting his forkèd sting into his claws,   10
  Privily shed his poison through his bones,
  Which made him swell, that there his bowels burst,
  That did so much in his own greatness trust.
  So Humber, having conquered Albanact,
  Doth yield his glory unto Locrine's sword.   15
  Mark what ensues and you may easily see,
  That all our life is but a tragedy.   [*Exit.*]

SCENE II

Enter LOCRINE, GUENDOLINE, CORINEUS, ASSARACUS, THRA-
          SIMACHUS, CAMBER.

Loc. And is this true? Is Albanactus slain?
  Hath cursèd Humber with his straggling host,
  With that his army made of mungrel curs,
  Brought our redoubted brother to his end?
  O that I had the Thracian Orpheus' harp   5
  For to awake out of the infernal shade
  Those ugly devils of black Erebus
  That might torment the damnèd traitor's soul;
  O that I had Amphion's instrument

17. *Exit.*] Rowe.

9-13.] Cf. "Visions of the worlds vanitie," ll.77-82:
  The subtill vermin creeping closely neare,
  Did in his drinke shed poyson priuilie;
  Which through his entrailes spredding diuersly,
  Made him to swell, that nigh his bowells brust,
  And him enforst to yeeld the victorie,
  That did so much in his owne greatnesse trust.
  17.] Cf. "The Teares of the Muses," 1.157: "For all mans life me seemes a Tragedy."

  III,ii,2. *straggling*] wandering, vagrant.
  3. *mungrel*] obsolete form of mongrel (*O.E.D.*).
  4. *redoubted*] famous, renowned.
  5-7.] see Ovid, *Metamorphoses*, X.
  9-11.] Amphion raised the stones of the lower city of Thebes by playing on his lyre.

>   To quicken with his vital notes and tunes   10
>   The flinty joints of every stony rock,
>   By which the Scythians might be punishèd.
>   For, by the lightning of almighty Jone,
>   The Hun shall die, had he ten thousand lives;
>   And would to God he had ten thousand lives,   15
>   That I might with the arm-strong Hercules
>   Crop off so vile an Hydra's hissing heads.
>   But say me, cousin, for I long to hear
>   How Albanact came by untimely death.
> *Thra.*   After the traiterous host of Scythians   20
>   Entered the field with martial equipage,
>   Young Albanact, impatient of delay,
>   Led forth his army 'gainst the straggling mates,
>   Whose multitude did daunt our soldiers' minds.
>   Yet nothing could dismay the forward prince,   25
>   But with a courage most heroical,
>   Like to a lion 'mongst a flock of lambs,
>   Made havoc of the faint-heart fugitives,
>   Hewing a passage through them with his sword.
>   Yea, we had almost given them the repulse,   30
>   When suddenly from out the silent wood,
>   Hubba, with twenty thousand soldiers,
>   Cowardly came upon our weakened backs,

---

  16. *arm...Hercules*] Cf. *Selimus*, 1.1671: "...arme-strong son of *Ioue*"; both plays were probably influenced by Greene's *Menaphon*, "...as if another *Alcides* (the arme-strong darling of the doubled night) by wrastling with snakes..." (Alexander B. Grosart, ed., *The Life and Complete Works...of Robert Greene* (New York: Russell & Russell, 1964), VI,89).
  16-17.] Hercules' second labour was to kill the Lernaean Hydra, which had the body of a dog and many snaky heads, one of which was immortal; when Hercules cut off one head, three more replaced it, but he was able to overcome the monster by searing the roots of the severed head with burning branches, thus stopping the flow of blood and preventing the growth of a new head. Finally, he was able to cut off the immortal head (Robert Graves, *The Greek Myths*, II,108).
  18. *say me*] i.e., say to me (see Abbott, sec. 201).
  23. *mates*] companions, in a contemptuous sense.

And murdered all with fatal massacre;
Amongst the which old Debon, martial knight,   35
With many wounds was brought unto the death.
And Albanact, oppressed with multitude,
Whilst valiantly he felled his enemies,
Yielded his life and honour to the dust;
He being dead, the soldiers fled amain,   40
And I alone escapèd them by flight
To bring you tidings of these accidents.

Loc. Not agèd Priam, king of stately Troy,
Grand emperor of barbarous Asia,
When he beheld his noble-minded sons   45
Slain traitorously by all the Myrmidons,
Lamented more than I for Albanact.

Guen. Not Hecuba, the queen of Ilium,
When she beheld the town of Pergamus,
Her palace burnt with all-devouring flames,   50
Her fifty sons and daughters, fresh of hue,
Murdered by wicked Pyrrhus' bloody sword,
Shed such sad tears as I for Albanact.

Cam. The grief of Niobe, fair Athens' queen,

---

40. *amain*] at full speed.
42. *accidents*] events.
43-57.] Each of the speakers uses the "outbidding topos"; the classical figures most often referred to in the lament were Priam, Hecuba and Niobe (Clemen, *English Tragedy*, pp. 230-32). This choric lament occurs also in *Troades* (IV,i), *David and Bethsabe* (11.991 ff.) and *Tamburlaine, Part II*, III,ii,47-52 (Wolfgang Clemen, *A Commentary on Shakespeare's Richard III*, trans. Jean Bonheim (London: Methuen, 1968), p. 186).
46. *Myrmidons*] soldiers of Achilles.
48. *Hecuba*] wife of Priam and queen of Troy.
49. *Pergamus*] holy place of Troy.
52. *Pyrrhus*] son of Achilles.
54. *Niobe*] boasted that she was fairer than Latona, and, as a consequence, Niobe's sons and daughters were killed (Ovid, *Metamorphoses*, VI).
54. *Athens'*] Niobe was not the queen of Athens; Malone makes the interesting suggestion that the text should be emended to "Amphion's," but it seems unlikely that the compositor is in error here.

	For her seven sons, magnanimous in field,	55
	For her seven daughters, fairer than the fairest,	
	Is not to be compared with my laments.	
Cor.	In vain you sorrow for the slaughtered prince,	
	In vain you sorrow for his overthrow;	
	He loves not most that doth lament the most,	60
	But he that seeks to 'venge the injury.	
	Think you to quell the enemy's warlike train	
	With childish sobs and womanish laments?	
	Unsheath your swords, unsheath your conquering swords,	
	And seek revenge, the comfort for this sore.	65
	In Cornwall, where I hold my regiment,	
	Even just ten thousand valiant men-at-arms	
	Hath Corineus ready at command:	
	All these and more, if need shall more require,	
	Hath Corineus ready at command.	70
Cam.	And in the fields of martial Cambria,	
	Close by the boisterous Iscan's silver streams,	
	Where lightfoot fairies skip from bank to bank,	
	Full twenty thousand brave courageous knights,	
	Well exercised in feats of chivalry,	75
	In manly manner most invincible,	
	Young Camber hath with gold and victual;	
	All these and more, if need shall more require,	
	I offer up to 'venge my brother's death.	
Loc.	Thanks, loving uncle, and good brother too;	80
	For this revenge, for this sweet word, revenge,	
	Must ease and cease thy wrongful injuries;	
	And by the sword of bloody Mars I swear,	

---

55. magnanimous] *F*; magnimious *Q*.   64. conquering swords] *Rowe*; conquering sword *Q*.   73. fairies] *F*; faires *Q*.   81. word, revenge,] *M*; word revenge *Q*.

---

66. *regiment*] rule.
67. *just*] exactly.
71. *Cambria*] Wales.
72. *Iscan*] the river Usk in South Wales.

SC. II]   TRAGEDY OF LOCRINE   91

    Ne'er shall sweet quiet enter this my front,
    Till I be 'vengèd on his traitorous head   85
    That slew my noble brother Albanact.
    Sound drums and trumpets; muster up the camp,
    For we will straight march to Albania.   *Exeunt.*

SCENE III

Enter HUMBER, ESTRILD, HUBBA, TRUSSIER *and the soldiers.*

Hum. Thus are we come, victorious conquerors,
    Unto the flowing current's silver streams,
    Which, in memorial of our victory,
    Shall be agnominated by our name,
    And talkèd of by our posterity.   5
    For sure I hope before the golden sun
    Posteth his horses to fair Thetis' plains
    To see the waters turnèd into blood,
    And change his bluish hue to rueful red,
    By reason of the fatal massacre   10
    Which shall be made upon the virent plains.
        Enter the Ghost *of* ALBANACT.
Gho. See how the traitor doth presage his harm;
    See how he glories at his own decay;
    See how he triumphs at his proper loss;
    O Fortune vile, unstable, fickle, frail!   15

III,iii,11.1   ALBANACT] *F*; Almanact *Q*.   12. *Gho.*] *add. Rowe*; not in *Q*.

---

    88. *Albania*] Scotland.

    III,iii,3.] In all other accounts, the river is named as a memorial to Humber's defeat and death.
    4. *agnominated*] agnominate is an obsolete term meaning to nickname; *Locrine* cited by the *O.E.D.*
    7. *Thetis*] a sea nymph.
    11. *virent*] verdant.

Hum. Methinks I see both armies in the field;
   The broken lances climb the crystal skies,
   Some headless lie, some breathless on the ground,
   And every place is strawed with carcasses;
   Behold, the grass hath lost his pleasant green,   20
   The sweetest sight that ever might be seen.
Gho. Ay, traitorous Humber, thou shalt find it so;
   Yea, to thy cost thou shalt the same behold,
   With anguish, sorrow, and with sad laments.
   The grassy plains that now do please thine eyes,   25
   Shall ere the night be coloured all with blood;
   The shady groves which now enclose thy camp
   And yield sweet savours to thy damnèd corpse,
   Shall ere the night be figured all with blood;
   The profound stream that passeth by thy tents,   30
   And with his moisture serveth all thy camp,
   Shall ere the night converted be to blood,
   Yea, with the blood of those thy straggling boys;
   For now revenge shall ease my lingering grief,
   And now revenge shall glut my longing soul.   35
Hub. Let come what will, I mean to bear it out,
   And either live with glorious victory,
   Or die with fame renowned for chivalry.
   He is not worthy of the honeycomb
   That shuns the hives because the bees have stings;   40
   That likes me best that is not got with ease,

---

19. And] *F*; Anb *Q*.   38. renowned] *M*; renowmed *Q*; renown'd *F*.

---

   19. *strawed*] covered (*O.E.D.*, straw, $v.^1$, 2, *Obs*.).
   20. *his*] used as the genitive of "it" (Abbott, sec. 228).
   28. *corpse*] a living body.
   29. *figured*] patterned.
   34-35.] classical belief that the ghost of the dead man cannot rest until his death is revenged.
   39-40.] proverbial (Tilley H556,"No Honey without gall"); cf. *Selimus*, 11.824-25: "Because the bees haue stings with them alway,/ To fare our mouthes in honie to embay."

SC. III]   TRAGEDY OF LOCRINE   93

      Which thousand dangers do accompany;
      For nothing can dismay our regal mind,
      Which aims at nothing but a golden crown,
      The only upshot of mine enterprises.   45
      Were they enchanted in grim Pluto's court,
      And kept for treasure 'mongst his hellish crew,
      I would either quell the triple Cerberus
      And all the army of his hateful hags,
      Or roll the stone with wretched Sisyphus.   50
Hum. Right martial be thy thoughts, my noble son,
      And all thy words savour of chivalry.
             [*Enter* SEGAR, *hastily.*]
      But, warlike Segar, what strange accidents
      Makes you to leave the warding of the camp?
Seg. To arms, my lord, to honourable arms,   55
      Take helm and targe in hand; the Britons come
      With greater multitude than erst the Greeks

50. Sisyphus] *Hazlitt*; Sisiphon *Q*.   52.1. *Enter* SEGAR, *hastily.*] *Moltke.*

44-45.] Cf. *Tamburlaine, Part I*, II,vii,26-29: "...never rest,/ Until we reach the ripest fruit of all,/ That perfect bliss and sole felicity,/ The sweet fruition of an earthly crown."
   45. *upshot*] "end aimed at"; *Locrine* cited in the *O.E.D.* (sb., 2, *Obs.*).
   46-50.] Hubba uses a literary formula; he will seek the crown even if it is placed in a "dreadful landscape"--cf. *Tamburlaine, Part II*, I,iv,79-84 (Riggs, *Heroical Histories*, p. 76).
   50. *Sisyphus*] condemned to push a stone up a mountain in hell, only to have it roll back down (Ovid, *Metamorphoses*, IV).
   53. *accidents*] i.e., happenings by chance.
   54. *Makes*] third person plural often ends in "s" (see Abbott, sec. 333).
   54. *warding*] "guarding"; *Locrine* cited in the *O.E.D.* (vbl. sb.^{1}, 1).
   55-56. *To...hand*] Cf. Peele, "A Farewell," 1.11, "Your Rests and Muskets take, take Helme and Targe," and 1.50, "To Armes, to Armes, to honourable Armes."
   57. *erst*] once.

94   TRAGEDY OF LOCRINE   [ACT III

         Brought to the ports of Phrygian Tenedos.
Hum. But what saith Segar to these accidents?
         What counsel gives he in extremities?   60
Seg. Why this, my lord, experience teacheth us:
         That resolution is a sole help at need.
         And this, my lord, our honour teacheth us:
         That we be bold in every enterprise.
         Then since there is no way but fight or die,   65
         Be resolute, my lord, for victory.
Hum. And resolute, Segar, I mean to be.
         Perhaps some blissful star will favour us,
         And comfort bring to our perplexèd state.
         Come, let us in and fortify our camp,   70
         So to withstand their strong invasion.   Exeunt.

                            SCENE IV

        Enter STRUMBO, TROMPART, OLIVER and his son WILLIAM
                          following them.

Strum. Nay, neighbour Oliver, if you be so hot, come,
         prepare yourself; you shall find two as stout
         fellows of us as any in all the North.
Oliv. No, by my dorth, neighbour Strumbo. Ich zee dat

58. Tenedos] F; Tenidos Q.   III,iv,1.] hot] Simms; whot Q.

---

   58. *Tenedos*] "A small island in the Aegean Sea situated...on the
NW coast of Asia Minor...The Greeks landed in Tenedos on their way
to Troy, killed Tenes, and ravaged the island. It was to this
island that the Greeks withdrew when they left the Wooden Horse on
the beach at Troy to delude the Trojans into the belief that they had
sailed for home" (*The New Century Classical Handbook*, ed. Catherine
B. Avery (New York: Appleton-Century-Crofts, Inc., 1962), p. 1063).

   III,iv,4-10.] Comic characters often use the rustic dialects of
the south and southwest (close to present dialects in Somerset, Dor-
set, Devon); they are characterized by voicing initial fricatives,
e.g., [f,s,ʃ] become [v,z,], by saying [θr] as [dr] and by saying
"ich" for "I" (Helge Kökeritz, *Shakespeare's Pronunciation* (New Haven:
Yale University Press, 1953), p. 36).
   4. *by...dorth*] "by my troth" (Malone); "dorth" not recorded in
the *O.E.D.*

SC. IV] TRAGEDY OF LOCRINE 95

        you are a man of small 'zideration, dat will zeek 5
        to injure your old vreends, one of your vamiliar
        guests, and derefore zeeing your 'pinion is to deal
        withouten reazon, Ich and my zon, William, will take
        dat course, dat shall be fardest vrom reason. How
        zay you? will you have my daughter or no? 10
Strum. A very hard question, neighbour, but I will solve
        it as I may. What reason have you to demand it of
        me?
Will. Marry, Sir, what reason had you, when my sister
        was in the barn, to tumble her upon the hay, and 15
        to fish her belly?
Strum. Mass, thou sayest true. Well, but would you have
        me marry her therefore? No, I scorn her, and you,
        and you; ay, I scorn you all.
Oliv. You will not have her then? 20
Strum. No, as I am a true gentleman.
Will. Then will we school you, ere you and we part
        hence. [*They fight.*]
Enter MARGERY *and snatch the staff out of her brother's*
        hand as he is fighting.
Strum. Ay, you come in pudding-time, or else I had
        dressed them. 25
Mar. You, Master Saucebox, Lobcock, Cockscomb, you,
        Slopsauce, lickfingers, will you not hear?

---

23. *They fight.*] M.

---

  16. *tumble...belly*] Malone points to a similar allusion in *Wint.*, I,ii,194-95: "...she has been sluic'd in's absence/ And his pond fish'd by his next neighbour..."
  17. *Mass*] "by the mass" was a common oath.
  24. *pudding-time*] the time when puddings are to be had; hence, an opportune moment.
  25. *dressed*] given a beating to; also, a pun on the preparation of food (*O.E.D.*, dress, *v.*, 9 and 13.a).
  26. *Saucebox*] person addicted to making saucy remarks.
  26. *Lobcock*] "country bumpkin"; cf. *Ralph Roister Doister*, III, iii,44: "Ye are...Such a lilburne, such a hoball, such a lobcocke" (*O.E.D.*).

Strum. Who speak you to? me?

Mar. Ay, Sir, to you, John Lackhonesty, Littlewit. Is it you that will have none of me? 30

Strum. No, by my troth, Mistress Nicebice. How fine you can nickname me. I think you were brought up in the University of Bridewell; you have your rhetoric so ready at your tongue's end, as if you were never well warned when you were young. 35

Mar. Why then, Goodman Codshead, if you will have none of me, farewell.

Strum. If you be so plain, Mistress Driggle-draggle, fare you well.

Mar. Nay, Master Strumbo, ere you go from hence we must have more words. You will have none of me? 40

They both fight.

Strum. O, my head, my head! Leave, leave, leave! I will, I will, I will!

Mar. Upon that condition I let thee alone.

Oliv. How now, Master Strumbo, hath my daughter taught you a new lesson? 45

Strum. Ay, but hear you, Goodman Oliver, it will not be for my ease to have my head broken every day; therefore remedy this and we shall agree.

Oliv. Well, zon, well, for you are my zon now; all shall be remedied. Daughter, be friends with him. 50

Shake hands.

[*Exeunt* OLIVER, WILLIAM *and* MARGERY.]

Strum. You are a sweet nut; the devil crack you.
Masters, I think it be my luck. My first wife was a

---

34. you] *F*; your *Q*. 51.2. *Exeunt* OLIVER, WILLIAM *and* MARGERY.] *M*.

---

31. *Nicebice*] a "nicebecetur" is a "dainty, fine, or fashionable girl"; the sole occurrence of "Nicebice," according to the *O.E.D.*, is in *Locrine*.
33. *Bridewell*] a prison in London.
34-35. *as...young*] i.e., never scolded as a child.
36. *Codshead*] blockhead.

SC. IV] TRAGEDY OF LOCRINE 97

    loving quiet wench; but this, I think, would weary
    the devil. I would she might be burnt as my   55
    other wife was. If not, I must run to the halter
    for help. O, Codpiece, thou hast done thy master;
    this it is to be meddling with warm plackets. [*Exit.*]

SCENE V

Enter LOCRINE, CAMBER, CORINEUS, THRASIMACHUS, ASSARACUS.

Loc. Now am I guarded with an host of men,
    Whose haughty courage is invincible;
    Now am I hemmed with troops of soldiers,
    Such as might force Bellona to retire,
    And make her tremble at their puissance;   5
    Now sit I like the mighty god of war
    When armèd with his coat of adamant,
    Mounted his chariot drawn with mighty bulls,
    He drove the Argives over Xanthus' streams;
    Now, cursèd Humber, doth thy end draw nigh.   10
    Down goes the glory of his victories,
    And all his fame, and all his high renown
    Shall in a moment yield to Locrine's sword;
    Thy bragging banners crossed with argent streams,
    The ornaments of thy pavilions   15
    Shall all be captivated with this hand;
    And thou thyself at Albanactus' tomb

---

58. *Exit.*] This ed.; *Exeunt. Q.* III,v,0.1. ASSARACUS] *Hazlitt*;
Assarachus *Q.* 7. adamant] *F*; Adament *Q.*

---

  56. *halter*] gallows.
  57. *Codpiece...master*] i.e., sexual licence is his undoing.
  58. *plackets*] petticoats or the slits in a petticoat (Onions).

III,v,3. *hemmed with*] surrounded by.
  7. *adamant*] extremely hard stone (Onions); cf. *Selimus*, 1.2489:
"...Mars arm'd in his adamantiue coate."
  9. *Argives...streams*] refers to the Greeks being driven over a
river at Troy.
  14. *argent streams*] silvery lines or streaks.

                Shalt offered be, in satisfaction
                Of all the wrongs thou didst him when he lived.
                But canst thou tell me, brave Thrasimachus,   20
                How far we are distant from Humber's camp?
    Thra.   My lord, within yon foul accursèd grove
                That bears the tokens of our overthrow,
                This Humber hath intrenched his damnèd camp.
                March on, my lord, because I long to see   25
                The treacherous Scythians squeltering in their gore.
    Loc.   Sweet Fortune, favour Locrine with a smile,
                That I may 'venge my noble brother's death;
                And in the midst of stately Troynovant
                I'll build a temple to thy deity   30
                Of perfect marble and of jacinth stones,
                That it shall pass the high pyramidés,
                Which with their top surmount the firmament.
    Cam.   The arm-strong offspring of the doubted knight,
                Stout Hercules, Alcmena's mighty son,   35
                That tamed the monsters of the threefold world
                And rid the oppressèd from the tyrants' yokes,
                Did never show such valiantness in fight,
                As I will now for noble Albanact.
    Cor.   Full fourscore years hath Corineus lived,   40
                Sometime in war, sometime in quiet peace,
                And yet I feel myself to be as strong

22. yon] *Rowe*; your *Q*.   29. Troynovant] *Rowe*; Troinonant *Q*.

---

   19. *didst him*] Cf. *Ham.*, II,ii,610: "Who does me this?" (Abbott, sec. 220).
   26. *squeltering*] see note II,vii,4.
   31. *jacinth*] gem of a blue or reddish-orange colour.
   33. *firmament*] the sphere containing the fixed stars; the eighth heaven of the Ptolemaic system.
   34. *doubted*] redoubted; respected, feared.
   34-35.] Zeus begot Hercules by impersonating Alcmena's husband and lying with her one night which he extended to twice its usual length.
   36. *That*] see Abbott, sec. 260.

As erst I was in summer of mine age,
Able to toss this great unwieldy club,
Which hath been painted with my foemen's brains; 45
And with this club I'll break the strong array
Of Humber and his straggling soldiers,
Or lose my life amongst the thickest press,
And die with honour in my latest days;
Yet, ere I die, they all shall understand 50
What force lies in stout Corineus' hand.
Thra. And if Thrasimachus detract the fight,
Either for weakness, or for cowardice,
Let him not boast that Brutus was his eme,
Or that brave Corineus was his sire. 55
Loc. Then courage, soldiers, first for your safety,
Next for your peace, last for your victory. *Exeunt.*

[SCENE VI]

Sound the alarm. Enter HUBBA *and* SEGAR *at one door, and*
CORINEUS *at the other.*

Cor. Art thou that Humber, prince of fugitives,
That by thy treason slew'st young Albanact?
Hub. I am his son that slew young Albanact,
And if thou take not heed, proud Phrygian,
I'll send thy soul unto the Stygian lake, 5
There to complain of Humber's injuries.
Cor. You triumph, Sir, before the victory,
For Corineus is not so soon slain.

44. unwieldy] *Simms*; vnwildie *Q.* III,vi. SCENE VI] *Simms.*

---

52. detract...fight] i.e., withdraw from the fight (Steevens).
III,vi,0.1. at...door] i.e., at one side of the stage.
5. *Stygian lake*] in hell.

But, cursèd Scythians, you shall rue the day
That ere you came into Albania. 10
So perish they that envy Britain's wealth,
So let them die with endless infamy,
And he that seeks his sovereign's overthrow,
Would this my club might aggravate his woe.
Strikes them both down with his club. [*Exeunt fighting.*]

[SCENE VII]

Enter HUMBER

Hum. Where may I find some desert wilderness,
Where I may breathe out curses as I would,
And scare the earth with my condemning voice;
Where every echo's repercussion
May help me to bewail mine overthrow, 5
And aid me in my sorrowful laments?
Where may I find some hollow uncouth rock,
Where I may damn, condemn and ban my fill
The heavens, the hell, the earth, the air, the fire,
And utter curses to the concave sky, 10
Which may infect the airy regions,

---

11. they that] *F*; that they *Q*.   14.1. Exeunt fighting.] *Moltke*.
III,vii.   SCENE VII] *Simms*.   2. breathe] *F*; breath *Q*.

III,vii,1-35.] What begins as a "speech of mourning" becomes one of execration at 1.7; it includes an "invocation to the furies," one of the commonplaces of the lament (see Clemen, *English Tragedy,* pp. 243-44).
    7-9.] Cf. *Battle of Alcazar,* V,i,1268-71:
        Where shall I finde some unfrequented place,
        Some uncouth walke where I may curse my fill,
        My starres, my dam, my planets and my nurse,
        The fire, the aire, the water, and the earth.
(Gaud, "Authorship of *Locrine,*" p. 421).
    8. *ban*] curse.
    10-11.] Cf. *Selimus,* 11.1804-5: "And vtter curses to the concaue skie,/ Which may infect the regions of the ayre."

SC. VII]   TRAGEDY OF LOCRINE   101

And light upon the Briton Locrine's head?
You ugly sprites that in Cocytus mourn,
And gnash your teeth with dolorous laments;
You fearful dogs that in black Lethe howl,   15
And scare the ghosts with your wide open throats;
You ugly ghosts that, flying from these dogs,
Do plunge yourselves in Puryflegiton;
Come, all of you, and with your shrieking notes
Accompany the Britons' conquering host.   20
Come, fierce Erinnys, horrible with snakes;
Come, ugly Furies, armèd with your whips;
You threefold judges of black Tartarus,
And all the army of you hellish fiends,
With new-found torments rack proud Locrine's bones! 25
O gods and stars, damned be the gods and stars
That did not drown me in fair Thetis' plains.
Curst be the sea that with outrageous waves,
With surging billows did not rive my ships
Against the rocks of high Ceraunia,   30
Or swallow me into her wat'ry gulf;
Would God we had arrived upon the shore
Where Polyphemus and the Cyclops dwell,

15. You] *F*; Yea *Q*.   20. Accompany] *F*; Accompaie *Q*.   25. Locrine's] *Simms*; Locrins *Q*.   30. Ceraunia] *Simms*; Cerannia *Q*.   31. swallow] *M*; swallowed *Q*.   33. Polyphemus] *F2*; Poliphlemus *Q*.

---

13. *Cocytus*] river in hell.
15. *Lethe*] river in hell, the drinking of whose waters caused forgetfulness.
18. *Puryflegiton*] Phlegethon, a river in hell that always burns.
21. *Erinnys*] the Furies; see note I,ii,256.
21.] Cf. *Selimus*, 1.1319: "The pitilesse *Erymnies* arm'd with whippes."
23. *threefold judges*] see note, I,ii,237.
28. *outrageous*] enormous.
30. *Ceraunia*] a range of mountains in the eastern part of the Caucasus system.
33. *Polyphemus*] one of the Cyclops, a race of one-eyed giants; blinded by Ulysses.

>   Or where the bloody Anthropophagi
>   With greedy jaws devours the wandering wights.   35
>   *Enter the* Ghost *of* ALBANACT.
>   But why comes Albanact's bloody ghost,
>   To bring a corsive to our miseries?
>   Is't not enough to suffer shameful flight,
>   But we must be tormented now with ghosts,
>   With apparitions fearful to behold?   40
> *Gho.*   Revenge, revenge for blood!
> *Hum.*   So naught will satisfy your wandering ghost
>   But dire revenge, nothing but Humber's fall,
>   Because he conquered you in Albany.
>   Now, by my soul, Humber would be condemned   45
>   To Tantal's hunger or Ixion's wheel,
>   Or to the vulture of Prometheus,
>   Rather than that this murder were undone.
>   Whenas I die, I'll drag thy cursèd ghost
>   Through all the rivers of foul Erebus,   50
>   Through burning sulphur of the Limbo-lake,
>   To allay the burning fury of that heat
>   That rageth in mine everlasting soul.
> *Gho.*   *Vindicta! vindicta!*   *Exeunt.*

34. Anthropophagi] *Simms*; Anthropomphagie *Q.*   44. Albany] *F*;
Vlbany *Q.*   54. Exeunt.] *Hazlitt*; after 53 *Q.*

---

    34. *Anthropophagi*] "cannibals" (Onions); cf. *Selimus*, 11. 1420-21:
"More bloodie then the *Anthropomphagi*,/ That fill their hungry
stomachs with mans flesh."
    37. *corsive*] obsolete form of "corrosive" meaning that which
causes annoyance, and, thus, increases the misery (*O.E.D.*, corrosive,
sb., 3).
    46. *Tantal*] Tantalus; see note I,ii,250.
    46. *Ixion*] bound to a wheel in hell and condemned to revolve
eternally.
    47. *Prometheus*] He was chained by Zeus and a vulture (in some
versions an eagle) tore at his liver every day; his crime is
described by Hesiod (*Theogony*, 534 ff.) as his deceit concerning
sacrifices to the gods and by Aeschylus (*Prometheus Bound*, 7 ff.) as
the theft of fire from the gods in order to give it to mortal men
(*O.C.D.*).
    51. *Limbo*] the first region of Tartarus where those souls went
who were neither virtuous nor evil.
    54. *Vindicta*] revenge.

ACT IV

SCENE I

Enter ATE *as before. Then let there follow* OMPHALE, *daughter to the king of Lydia, having a club in her hand, and a lion's skin on her back;* HERCULES *following with a distaff. Then let* OMPHALE *turn about, and taking off her pantofle, strike* HERCULES *on the head; then let them depart.* ATE *remaining, saying:*

Ate. *Quem non Argolici mandata severa tyranni,*
 Non potuit Juno vincere, vincit amor.
 Stout Hercules, the mirror of the world,
 Son to Alcmena and great Jupiter,
 After so many conquests won in field, 5
 After so many monsters quelled by force,
 Yielded his valiant heart to Omphale,
 A fearful woman, void of manly strength.
 She took the club and ware the lion's skin;
 He took the wheel and maidenly 'gan spin. 10
 So martial Locrine, cheered with victory,

---

9. wore] *F*; ware *Q*.

  0.4. *distaff*] represents "the type of women's work" (*O.E.D.*, 3).
  0.5. *pantofle*] slipper.
  1-2.] "He whom the tyrant's mandate could not move,/ Nor Juno's self subdue, submits to love" (Moltke); from Ovid, Epistle IX, *Heroides*, and quoted by Whitney (p. 63).
  3. *mirror*] paragon.
  7-10.] Cf. Seneca, *Hercules Oetaeus*, 11.280-283.

> Falleth in love with Humber's concubine,
> And so forgetteth peerless Guendoline.
> His uncle Corineus storms at this,
> And forceth Locrine for his grace to sue.   15
> Lo, here the sum; the process doth ensue.   *Exit.*

SCENE II

Enter LOCRINE, CAMBER, CORINEUS, ASSARACUS, THRASIMACHUS
and the soldiers.

Loc. Thus from the fury of Bellona's broils,
With sound of drum and trumpet's melody,
The Briton king returns triumphantly.
The Scythians slain with great occision
Do equalize the grass in multitude,   5
And with their blood have stained the streaming
   brooks,
Offering their bodies and their dearest blood
As sacrifice to Albanactus' ghost;
Now, cursèd Humber, hast thou paid thy due,
For thy deceits and crafty treacheries,   10
For all thy guiles and damnèd stratagems,
With loss of life and ever-during shame.
Where are thy horses trapped with burnished gold,
Thy trampling coursers ruled with foaming bits?
Where are thy soldiers, strong and numberless,   15
Thy valiant captains and thy noble peers?
Even as the country clowns with sharpest scythes
Do mow the withered grass from off the earth,

IV,ii,3. triumphantly] *F*; triumphanly *Q*.   6. blood] *F*; biood *Q*.

16. *process*] orderly enactment.

IV,ii,4. *occision*] slaughter; cf. *Selimus*, 1.2476: "The great occision which the victors make?"
5. *equalize...multitude*] match the individual blades of grass in number.
17-23.] a similar metaphor occurs in Lodge, *The Complaint of Elstred*, 11.145-148.

SC. II]   TRAGEDY OF LOCRINE

      Or as the ploughman with his piercing share
      Rendeth the bowels of the fertile fields,   20
      And rippeth up the roots with razors keen;
      So Locrine, with his mighty curtle-axe,
      Hath croppèd off the heads of all thy Huns;
      So Locrine's peers have daunted all thy peers,
      And drove thine host unto confusion   25
      That thou mayst suffer penance for thy fault,
      And die for murdering valiant Albanact.
Cor. And thus, yea thus, shall all the rest be served
      That seek to enter Albion 'gainst our wills.
      If the brave nation of the Troglodytes,   30
      If all the coal-black Ethiopians,
      If all the forces of the Amazons,
      If all the hosts of the barbarian lands,
      Should dare to enter this our little world,
      Soon should they rue their overbold attempts,   35
      That after us our progeny may say,
      There lie the beasts that sought to usurp our land.
Loc. Ay, they are beasts that seek to usurp our land,
      And like to brutish beasts they shall be served.
      For mighty Jove, the supreme king of heaven,   40
      That guides the concourse of the meteors,
      And rules the motion of the azure sky,
      Fights always for the Britons' safety.
      But stay, methinks I hear some shrieking noise,
      That draweth near to our pavilion.   45
          Enter the soldiers leading in ESTRILD.
Est. What prince soe'er, adorned with golden crown,

---

46. crown] *F; not in Q.*

  22. *curtle-axe*] a short, broad cutting sword.
  30. *Troglodytes*] "People in the furthest part of Affrike, beyonde Aethiope, whiche dwell in caues..." (Cooper).
  34. *this...world*] Cf. Gaunt in *R2*, II,i,45: "this little world."
  41. *concourse*] conjunction.
  46. *crown*] A word is obviously missing from the quarto text, and "crown" fits both the sense and the rhyme scheme.
  46-75.] organized into five stanzas, rhyming ababcc; see Introduction, p. 3.

Doth sway the regal sceptre in his hand,
And thinks no chance can ever throw him down,
Or that his state shall everlasting stand,
Let him behold poor Estrild in this plight, 50
The perfect platform of a troubled wight.
Once was I guarded with mavortial bands,
Compassed with princes of the noble blood;
Now am I fallen into my foemen's hands,
And with my death must pacify their mood. 55
O life, the harbour of calamities!
O death, the haven of all miseries!
I could compare my sorrows to thy woe,
Thou wretched queen of wretched Pergamus,
But that thou view'dst thy enemy's overthrow; 60
Nigh to the rock of high Caphareus,
Thou saw'st their death, and then departedst thence;
I must abide the victor's insolence.
The gods that pitied thy continual grief,
Transformed thy corpse, and with thy corpse thy care;
Poor Estrild lives despairing of relief, 65
For friends in trouble are but few and rare.
What, said I few? Ay, few or none at all,
For cruel Death made havoc of them all.
Thrice happy they whose fortune was so good 70

47. sceptre] *Simms*; sceptler *Q*; Scepter *F*. 52. mavortial] *Simms*; manortiall *Q*.

47.] wield the sceptre as an emblem of sovereignty.
51. *platform*] model.
52. *mavortial*] obsolete adjective meaning "warlike"; *Locrine* cited in the *O.E.D.*
55. *mood*] anger.
59.] see notes III,ii,48-49.
61. *Caphareus*] on the south-eastern shore of the island of Euboea (Greece). In Ovid's account (*Metamorphoses*, XIII), Hecuba takes her revenge in Thrace.
61-65.] In revenge for the death of her son, Polydorus, whose body washed up on the shore beneath her feet, Hecuba blinded Polymestor; before she could be captured she was transformed into a dog (Ovid, *Metamorphoses*, XIII).

SC. II] TRAGEDY OF LOCRINE 107

>   To end their lives, and with their lives their woes;
>   Thrice hapless I, whom Fortune so withstood,
>   That cruelly she gave me to my foes.
>   O, soldiers, is there any misery
>   To be compared to Fortune's treachery? 75
> *Loc.* Camber, this same should be the Scythian queen.
> *Cam.* So may we judge by her lamenting words.
> *Loc.* So fair a dame mine eyes did never see;
>   With floods of woes she seems o'erwhelmed to be.
> *Cam.* O Locrine, hath she not a cause for to be sad? 80
>   LOCRINE *at one side of the stage.*
> *Loc.* If she have cause to weep for Humber's death,
>   And shed salt tears for her overthrow,
>   Locrine may well bewail his proper grief;
>   Locrine may move his own peculiar woe.
>   He, being conquered, died a speedy death, 85
>   And felt not long his lamentable smart;
>   I, being conqueror, live a lingering life,
>   And feel the force of Cupid's sudden stroke.
>   I gave him cause to die a speedy death;
>   He left me cause to wish a speedy death. 90
>   O that sweet face, painted with nature's dye,
>   Those roseal cheeks mixed with a snowy white,
>   That decent neck surpassing ivory,
>   Those comely breasts which Venus well might spite,
>   Are like to snares which wily fowlers wrought, 95
>   Wherein my yielding heart is prisoner caught.
>   The golden tresses of her dainty hair,
>   Which shine like rubies glittering with the sun,
>   Have so entrapped poor Locrine's love-sick heart,
>   That from the same no way it can be won. 100

81. *Loc.*] *Tyrrell*; *not in Q.* 92. mixed] *Simms*; mizt *Q*; mixt *F.*
96. caught] *F*; cought *Q.*

---

92. *roseal*] rose-coloured.
93. *decent*] comely.

How true is that which oft I heard declared:
One dram of joy must have a pound of care.
Est. Hard is their fall, who from a golden crown
Are cast into a sea of wretchedness.
Loc. [*Aside*] Hard is their thrall, who by Cupid's frown
Are wrapped in waves of endless carefulness. 105
Est. O kingdom, object to all miseries.
Loc. [*Aside*] O love, the extrem'st of all extremities.
                            Let him go into his chair.
First Sold. My lord, in ransacking the Scythian tents,
I found this lady, and to manifest 110
That earnest zeal I bear unto your grace,
I here present her to your majesty.
Second Sold. He lies, my lord; I found the lady first,
And here present her to your majesty.
First Sold. Presumptuous villain, wilt thou take my
prize? 115
Second Sold. Nay, rather thou deprivest me of my right.
First Sold. Resign thy title, caitiff, unto me,
Or with my sword I'll pierce thy coward's loins.
Second Sold. Soft words, good Sir; 'tis not enough to
speak:
A barking dog doth seldom strangers bite. 120
Loc. Unreverent villains, strive you in our sight?
Take them hence, jailer, to the dungeon;
There let them lie and try their quarrel out.
But thou, fair princess, be no whit dismayed,
But rather joy that Locrine favours thee. 125
Est. How can he favour me that slew my spouse?

---

105. Aside] Hazlitt.   108. Aside] Hazlitt.   121. strive] *F*; sttiue *Q*.

102.] proverbial; *Locrine* cited by Tilley, D582.
103-108.] elaborate rhetorical device where stichomythia is organized into a rhyming stanza; see Introduction, p. 3.
120.] proverbial; Tilley, B85 ("Great Barkers are no biters").
126-146.] Cf. Richard's wooing of Anne, *R3*, I,ii.

Loc.	The chance of war, my love, took him from thee.	
Est.	But Locrine was the causer of his death.	
Loc.	He was an enemy to Locrine's state,	
	And slew my noble brother Albanact.	130
Est.	But he was linked to me in marriage bond,	
	And would you have me love his slaughterer?	
Loc.	Better to love, than not to live at all.	
Est.	Better to die renowned for chastity,	
	Than live with shame and endless infamy.	135
	What would the common sort report of me,	
	If I forget my love, and cleave to thee?	
Loc.	Kings need not fear the vulgar sentences.	
Est.	But ladies must regard their honest name.	
Loc.	Is it a shame to live in marriage bonds?	140
Est.	No, but to be a strumpet to a king.	
Loc.	If thou wilt yield to Locrine's burning love,	
	Thou shalt be queen of fair Albania.	
Est.	But Guendoline will undermine my state.	
Loc.	Upon mine honour thou shalt have no harm.	145
Est.	Then lo, brave Locrine, Estrild yields to thee;	
	And by the gods whom thou dost invocate,	
	By the dread ghost of thy deceasèd sire,	
	By thy right hand and by thy burning love,	
	Take pity on poor Estrild's wretched thrall.	150
Cor.	Hath Locrine then forgot his Guendoline,	
	That thus he courts the Scythian's paramour?	
	What, are the words of Brute so soon forgot?	
	Are my deserts so quickly out of mind?	
	Have I been faithful to thy sire, now dead?	155

133. love] *Simms*; live *Q*.   148. dread] *F*; dead *Q*.

133.] Editors are divided as to whether the line should be emended to read "Better to love" (Tyrrell) or left as a truism, "That it is better to live on any terms than to die" (Malone). McKerrow suggests "Better so live" or "Better to love." A similar idea occurs in *The Complaint of Elstred*, 1.504, "Twere better to loue and liue, than loath and die."
    138. *vulgar sentences*] public opinion.
    150. *thrall*] thraldom or bondage.

112 TRAGEDY OF LOCRINE [ACT IV

> My bowels cry, Humber, give us some meat. 15
> But wretched Humber can give you no meat;
> These foul accursèd groves afford no meat.
> This fruitless soil, this ground, brings forth no
>   meat.
> The gods, hard-hearted gods, yield me no meat:
> Then how can Humber give you any meat? 20
> [*Stands aside.*]

Enter STRUMBO *with a pitchfork, and a Scotch cap saying,*

Strum. How do you, masters, how do you? How have you
'scaped hanging this long time? I'faith I have
'scaped many a scouring this year, but I thank God
I have passed them all with a good coraggio,
coraggio, and my wife and I are in great love and 25
charity now, I thank my manhood and my strength; for
I will tell you, masters, upon a certain day at
night I came home, to say the very truth, with my
stomach full of wine, and ran up into the chamber
where my wife soberly sat rocking my little baby, 30
leaning her back against the bed, singing lullaby.
Now, when she saw me come with my nose foremost,
thinking that I had been drunk, as I was indeed,
snatched up a faggot-stick in her hand, and came
furiously marching towards me with a big face, as 35
though she would have eaten me at a bit, thundering
out these words unto me: "Thou drunken knave, where

20.1. *Stands aside.*] This ed.   33. had been] *F*; bin *Q*.

15-20.] example of "antistrophe" or "counterturn" where one word finishes several lines in succession (Puttenham, *English Poesie*, Bk. III, chap. xix).
  20.1. *Scotch cap*] woollen hat, "without a brim, and decorated with two tails or streamers"; *Locrine* cited in *O.E.D.*
  23. *scouring*] beating.
  24. *coraggio*] Italian word for courage.
  36. *at...bit*] obsolete phrase meaning "at one bite" (*O.E.D.*, bit, sb.[1], 1).
  37-38. *Thou...long*] Cf. *Selimus*, l.1892: "Sir knaue she cries, where haue you bin?"

hast thou been so long? I shall teach thee how to
benight me another time"; and so she began to play
knaves trumps. Now, although I trembled, fearing 40
she would set her ten commandments in my face, I ran
within her, and taking her lustily by the middle, I
carried her valiantly to the bed, and flinging her
upon it, flung myself upon her, and there I delight-
ed her so with the sport I made, that ever after 45
she would call me sweet husband, and so banished
brawling forever. And to see the goodwill of the
wench! She bought with her portion a yard of land,
and by that I am now become one of the richest men
in our parish. Well, masters, what's a clock? 50
It is now breakfast time; you shall see what meat I
have here for my breakfast.
    Let him sit down and pull out his victuals.
Hum. [*coming forward.*] Was ever land so fruitless as
   this land?
Was ever grove so graceless as this grove?
Was ever soil so barren as this soil? 55
O no, the land where hungry Famés dwelt
May no wise equalize this cursèd land;

41. I] *M*; not in *Q*. 53. *coming forward.*] This ed.

---

39. *benight*] deceive, with the implication of involving in moral darkness.
 39-40. *she...trumps*] She is holding the trump card, i.e., the faggot stick, and she is successful in chastising her knave, Strumbo.
 41. *ten commandments*] ten fingernails; proverbial (Tilley, C553, "The ten Commandments"). Cf. *Selimus*, 11.1881-82: "...in daily feare of the breach of my wiues ten-commandemens."
 41. *I*] Malone's emendation completes the parallelism with the rest of the sentence.
 42. *within*] i.e., "near enough to come to grips with" (*O.E.D.*, B. prep., 8.b).
 48. *portion*] dowry.
 48. *yard...land*] quarter of an acre.
 50. *what's a clock*] anachronistic for Strumbo to refer to a clock; to find out "what o'clock it is" also means "to know (discover) the real state of things" (*O.E.D.*, clock, sb.^{1}, 4).

No, even the climate of the torrid zone
Brings forth more fruit than this accursèd grove.
Ne'er came sweet Ceres, ne'er came Venus here;   60
Triptolemus, the god of husbandmen,
Ne'er sowed his seed in this foul wilderness.
The hunger-bitten dogs of Acheron,
Chased from the ninefold Puryflegiton,
Have set their footsteps in this damnèd ground.   65
The iron-hearted Furies, armed with snakes,
Scattered huge Hydras over all the plains,
Which have consumed the grass, the herbs, the trees,
Which have drunk up the flowing water springs.

      STRUMBO, *hearing his voice, shall start up and*
        put meat in his pocket, seeking to hide himself.

Thou great commander of the starry sky,   70
That guid'st the life of every mortal wight,
From the enclosures of the fleeting clouds
Rain down some food, or else I faint and die.
Pour down some drink, or else I faint and die.
                              [*Seeing* STRUMBO.]
O Jupiter, hast thou sent Mercury   75
In clownish shape to minister some food?
Some meat, some meat, some meat!

Strum. O, alas, Sir, ye are deceived. I am not Mercury;
   I am Strumbo.

---

70. om. *Hum.*] Hazlitt; *Hum.* Q.   74.1. *Seeing* STRUMBO.] Moltke.

---

  58. *torrid zone*] region of the earth between the tropics; the dramatist may have concentrated on the meaning of "torrid" as scorched or burned in order to arrive at his view of tropical infertility.
  60. *Ceres*] "goddess of agriculture" (Onions).
  63. *Acheron*] river in hell (Onions).
  64. *ninefold*] source for the nine branches of the river is unknown; see, also, IV,v,16 and V,vi,24.
  75. *Mercury*] in Roman mythology, the messenger of the gods. The clown, or Zanni, in the Commedia Dell' Arte "would impersonate Mercury by adjusting the feathers in his hat or by fitting his shoes as wings" (Lea, *Italian Popular Comedy*, II,400).

Hum. Give me some meat, villain; give me some meat, 80
    Or 'gainst this rock, I'll dash thy cursèd brains,
    And rent thy bowels with my bloody hands.
    Give me some meat, villain, give me some meat!
Strum. By the faith of my body, good fellow, I had
    rather give an whole ox than that thou shouldst 85
    serve me in that sort. Dash out my brains! O
    horrible, terrible! [*Aside*] I think I have a quarry
    of stones in my pocket.

Let him make as though he would give him some, and as he putteth out his hand, enter the Ghost *of* ALBANACT, *and strike him on the hand, and so* STRUMBO *runs out,* HUMBER
following him.

Gho. Lo, here the gift of fell ambition,
    Of usurpation and of treachery. 90
    Lo, here the harms that wait upon all those
    That do intrude themselves in others' lands
    Which are not under their dominion. *Exit.*

SCENE IV

Enter LOCRINE *alone.*

Loc. Seven years hath agèd Corineus lived
    To Locrine's grief and fair Estrilda's woe,
    And seven years more he hopeth yet to live.
    O, supreme Jove, annihilate this thought!
    Should he enjoy the air's fruition? 5
    Should he enjoy the benefit of life?
    Should he contemplate the radiant sun,

---

87. *Aside*] *Moltke.* 88.4. om. *Exit.*] *Hazlitt*; *Exit. Q.*
IV,iv,7. sun] *Simms*; sonne *Q*.

---

85. *an whole*] "an" was often used before consonants and vowels (Abbott, sec. 80).
89-93.] political moral; see Introduction, p. 22.

That makes my life equal to dreadful death?
Venus, convey this monster from the earth,
That disobeyeth thus thy sacred hests. 10
Cupid, convey this monster to dark hell,
That disannuls thy mother's sugared laws.
Mars, with thy target all beset with flames,
With murdering blade bereave him of his life
That hind'reth Locrine in his sweetest joys. 15
And yet, for all his diligent aspect,
His wrathful eyes, piercing like Lynceus' eyes,
Well have I overmatched his subtlety.
Nigh Durolitum, by the pleasant Lea,
Where brackish Thamis slides with silver streams, 20
Making a breach into the grassy downs,
A curious arch of costly marble fraught
Hath Locrine framèd underneath the ground;
The walls whereof, garnished with diamonds,
With ophirs, rubies, glistering emeralds, 25
And interlaced with sun-bright carbuncles,
Lighten the room with artificial day;
And from the Lea with water-flowing pipes
The moisture is derived into this arch,
Where I have placed fair Estrild secretly. 30
Thither eftsoons, accompanied with my page,
I covertly visit my heart's desire,
Without suspicion of the meanest eye,
For love aboundeth still with policy:

9. from] *F2*; fro *Q*. 13. with flames] *F*; wiih flames *Q*. 19. Durolitum] *Steevens*; Deucolitum *Q*. 19. Lea] *This ed.*; Lee *Q*. 24. garnished] *Simms*; garnish *Q*; garnisht *F*. 28. Lea] *This ed.*; Lee *Q*.

12. *mother's*] Venus'.
17. *Lynceus*] in Greek legend, renowned for keen sight.
19. *Durolitum*] town of Leyton in Essex (Steevens).
22. *curious*] skilfully wrought.
22. *fraught*] furnished.
25. *ophirs*] "Ophir" is the name of a region mentioned in Job 22: 24 where fine gold was obtained; hence, "ophirs" means pieces of gold.
26. *carbuncles*] "red or fiery precious stones" (Onions).
31. *eftsoons*] repeatedly.

SC. IV] TRAGEDY OF LOCRINE 117

  And thither still means Locrine to repair,   35
  Till Atropos cut off mine uncle's life.   *Exit.*

      SCENE V

   Enter HUMBER *alone, saying,*

Hum. *O vita misero longa, foelici brevis!*
  Eheu malorum fames extremum malum.
  Long have I livèd in this desert cave,
  With eating haws and miserable roots,
  Devouring leaves and beastly excrements.   5
  Caves were my beds and stones my pillowbears,
  Fear was my sleep, and horror was my dream,
  For still methought at every boisterous blast,
  Now Locrine comes, now, Humber, thou must die;
  So that for fear and hunger, Humber's mind   10
  Can never rest, but always trembling stands.
  O what Danubius now may quench my thirst?
  What Euphrates, what lightfoot Euripus,
  May now allay the fury of that heat,
  Which, raging in my entrails, eats me up?   15
  You ghastly devils of the ninefold Styx,
  You damnèd ghosts of joyless Acheron,

IV,v,1. foelici] *F*; faelici *Q*. 2. Eheu malorum] *F*; Ehen malorem *Q*.
15. entrails] *Rowe*; entralls *Q*.

IV,v,1-2.] "O life, long to the wretched--to the happy, short,/ Alas! of all evils, hunger is the worst" (Moltke).
 1.] motto used by Thomas Lodge on the title-page of *The Wounds of Civil War*.
 4. *haws*] fruit of the hawthorn.
 5. *excrements*] outgrowths, especially hair, nails, feathers; consisting largely of matter useless for nutrition.
 6. *pillowbears*] pillow-cases; i.e., pillows.
 13. *Euripus*] strait between the Greek island of Euboea and the mainland.
 16. *Styx*] river on the boundary of Tartarus.

You mournful souls, vexed in Abyssus' vaults,
You coal-black devils of Avernus' pond,
Come, with your flesh-hooks, rent my famished arms, 20
These arms that have sustained their master's life;
Come with your razors, rip my bowels up,
With your sharp fire-forks crack my starvèd bones;
Use me as you will, so Humber may not live.
Accursèd gods that rule the starry poles, 25
Accursèd Jove, king of the cursèd gods,
Cast down your lightning on poor Humber's head
That I may leave this deathlike life of mine.
What, hear you not? and shall not Humber die?
Nay, I will die, though all the gods say nay. 30
And, gentle Aby, take my troubled corpse,
Take it and keep it from all mortal eyes,
That none may say, when I have lost my breath,
The very floods conspired 'gainst Humber's death.
      Fling himself into the river.
   Enter the Ghost *of* ALBANACT.
Gho. En caedem sequitur, caedes in caede quiesco. 35
 Humber is dead! Joy heavens, leap earth, dance
  trees!
Now mayst thou reach thy apples, Tantalus,
And with them feed thy hunger-bitten limbs.
Now, Sisyphus, leave tumbling of thy rock,
And rest thy restless bones upon the same. 40
Unbind Ixion, cruel Rhadamanth,
And lay proud Humber on the whirling wheel.
Back will I post to hell-mouth Taenarus,
And pass Cocytus to the Elysian fields,
And tell my father Brutus of these news. *Exit.* 45

---

 18. *Abyssus*] "A depenes without bottome" (Cooper).
 19. *Avernus' pond*] reputed to be a lake of great depth that led to Hades (*O.C.D.*).
 31. *Aby*] Humber river; see note II,vii,25.
 35.] "Lo! death to death succeeds--in death I rest" (Moltke).
 43. *Taenarus*] or Taenarum, a cave on the southern tip of the Peloponnesus, where Hercules pulled Cerberus up from Hades (*O.C.D.*).

ACT V

SCENE I

Enter ATE *as before.* JASON, *leading* Creon's Daughter; MEDEA *following, hath a garland in her hand, and putting it on* Creon's Daughter's *head, setteth it on fire, and then, killing* JASON *and her, departeth.*

Ate. *Non tam Trinacriis exaestuat Aetna cavernis,*
 Laesae furtivo quam cor mulieris amore.
 Medea, seeing Jason leave her love
 And choose the daughter of the Theban king,
 Went to her devilish charms to work revenge;   5
 And raising up the triple Hecate,
 With all the rout of the condemnèd fiends,
 Framèd a garland by her magic skill,
 With which she wrought Jason and Creon's ill.
 So Guendoline, seeing herself misused,   10
 And Humber's paramour possess her place,
 Flies to the dukedom of Cornubia,
 And with her brother, stout Thrasimachus,
 Gathering a power of Cornish soldiers,

1. *Trinacriis exaestuat*] F; *Tincriis excestuat* Q.

1-2.] "Not with such tumult, in Sicilia's caves,/ Does Aetna rage, as doth the woman's heart,/ When rous'd to madness by clandestine fires!" (Moltke).
 6. *triple Hecate*] goddess of enchantments with the triple identity of Hecate, Luna and Diana.
 8-9.] Medea sent the garland to Creon's daughter as a wedding gift, and it burst into flames when she placed it on her head.

Gives battle to her husband and his host 15
Nigh to the river of great Mercia.
The chances of this dismal massacre
That which ensueth shortly will unfold. *Exit.*

SCENE II

Enter LOCRINE, CAMBER, ASSARACUS, THRASIMACHUS.

Assar. But tell me, cousin, died my brother so?
  Now who is left to helpless Albion
  That as a pillar might uphold our state,
  That might strike terror to our daring foes?
  Now who is left to hapless Brittany, 5
  That might defend her from the barbarous hands
  Of those that still desire her ruinous fall,
  And seek to work her downfall and decay?
Cam. Ay, uncle, death is our common enemy,
  And none but death can match our matchless power; 10
  Witness the fall of Albioneus' crew,
  Witness the fall of Humber and his Huns;
  And this foul death hath now increased our woe,
  By taking Corineus from this life,
  And in his room leaving us worlds of care. 15
Thra. But none may more bewail his mournful hearse
  Than I that am the issue of his loins.
  Now foul befall that cursèd Humber's throat
  That was the causer of his lingering wound.
Loc. Tears cannot raise him from the deal again. 20

16. Mercia] *Rowe*; Mertia *Q.*
V,ii,0.1. ASSARACUS] *Hazlitt*; Assarachus *Q.* 1. my] *F*; by *Q.*

---

16. *Mercia*] Midland region (Tatlock, *Legendary History*, p. 23).

V.ii.11. *Albioneus' crew*] giants that inhabited Britain before the arrival of Brutus; see note I,ii,116.

SC. II]   TRAGEDY OF LOCRINE   121

        But where's my lady, Mistress Guendoline?
Thra.   In Cornwall, Locrine, is my sister now,
        Providing for my father's funeral.
Loc.   And let her there provide her mourning weeds,
        And mourn forever her own widowhood.   25
        Ne'er shall she come within our palace gate,
        To countercheck brave Locrine in his love.
        Go, boy, to Durolitum, down the Ley,
        Unto the arch where lovely Estrild lies.
        Bring her and Sabren straight unto the court;   30
        She shall be queen in Guendolina's room.
        Let others wail for Corineus' death;
        I mean not so to macerate my mind,
        For him that barred me from my heart's desire.
Thra.   Hath Locrine then forsook his Guendoline?   35
        Is Corineus' death so soon forgot?
        If there be gods in heaven, as sure there be,
        If there be fiends in hell, as needs there must,
        They will revenge this thy notorious wrong,
        And pour their plagues upon thy cursèd head.   40
Loc.   What, prat'st thou, peasant, to thy sovereign?
        Or art thou strooken in some ecstasy?
        Dost thou not tremble at our royal looks?
        Dost thou not quake when mighty Locrine frowns?
        Thou beardless boy, were't not that Locrine scorns   45
        To vex his mind with such a heartless child,

---

28. Durolitum] *Steevens*; Deucolitum *Q*.   28. Ley] *Steevens*; Lee *Q*.

---

   33. *macerate*] waste away (*O.E.D.*, *v.*, 2); cf. Spenser, "Virgils Gnat," 11.94-95: "...sad cares, as wont to macerate/ And rend the greedie mindes of couetous men."
   41.] Cf. *Edward I*, xii,1975: "Why how now princockes, pratest thou to a king?" (Gaud, "Authorship of *Locrine*," p. 421).
   42. *strooken*] stricken; "to fall suddenly in...amazement" (*O.E.D.*, strike, *v.*, 47.b, *Obs.*).
   42. *ecstasy*] state of being beside oneself with passion.
   45. *beardless boy*] Thrasimachus seems to have become younger; Baldwin Maxwell suggests that a revision of the play has resulted in the combination of two characters into that of Thrasimachus (*Shakespeare Apocrypha*, p. 41). See Introduction, p. 31.

With the sharp point of this my battle-axe
I would send thy soul to Puriflegiton.
Thra. Though I be young and of a tender age,
    Yet will I cope with Locrine when he dares.   50
    My noble father with his conquering sword
    Slew the two giants, kings of Aquitaine.
    Thrasimachus is not so degenerate
    That he should fear and tremble at the looks
    Or taunting words of a venerean squire.   55
Loc. Menacest thou thy royal sovereign?
    Uncivil, not beseeming such as you,
    Injurious traitor, for he is no less
    That at defiance standeth with his king,
    Leave these thy taunts, leave these thy bragging
        words,   60
    Unless thou mean to leave thy wretched life.
Thra. If princes stain their glorious dignity
    With ugly spots of monstrous infamy,
    They leese their former estimation,
    And throw themselves into a hell of hate.   65
Loc. Wilt thou abuse my gentle patience,
    As though thou didst our high displeasure scorn?
    Proud boy, that thou mayst know thy prince is moved,
    Yea, greatly moved at this thy swelling pride,
    We banish thee forever from our court.   70
Thra. Then, losel Locrine, look unto thyself;
    Thrasimachus will 'venge this injury.   *Exit.*
Loc. Farewell, proud boy, and learn to use thy tongue.

---

    52. *two...Aquitaine*] Thrasimachus confuses his father's enemies--
the French kings were not giants. Maxwell points to this confusion
as further evidence of revision (*Shakespeare Apocrypha*, p. 42).
    55. *venerean squire*] a gallant or lover influenced by Venus and,
thus, inclined to wantonness.
    62-63.] a similar moral is drawn in *The Faerie Queene*, II,x,17:
"And fell to vaine voluptuous disease:/ He lou'd faire Ladie *Estrild*,
lewdly lou'd."
    64. *leese*] lose; obsolete form (*O.E.D.*).
    71. *losel*] worthless.
    73. *use*] employ for a desired end, i.e., to Locrine's advantage.

SC. II]   TRAGEDY OF LOCRINE   123

Assar. Alas, my lord, you should have called to mind
 The latest words that Brutus spake to you: 75
 How he desired you, by the obedience
 That children ought to bear unto their sire,
 To love and favour Lady Guendoline.
 Consider this, that if the injury
 Do move her mind, as certainly it will,   80
 War and dissension follows speedily.
 What though her power be not so great as yours?
 Have you not seen a mighty elephant
 Slain by the biting of a silly mouse?
 Even so the chance of war inconstant is.   85
Loc. Peace, uncle, peace and cease to talk hereof;
 For he that seeks, by whispering this or that,
 To trouble Locrine in his sweetest life,
 Let him persuade himself to die the death.
   Enter the Page, *with* ESTRILD *and* SABREN.
Est. O say me, Page, tell me, where is the king?   90
 Wherefore doth he send for me to the court?
 Is it to die? is it to end my life?
 Say me, sweet boy; tell me and do not feign.
Page. No, trust me, madam; if you will credit the
 little honesty that is yet left me, there is no   95
 such danger as you fear. But prepare yourself;
 yonder's the king.
Est. Then, Estrild, lift thy dazzled spirits up,
 And bless that blessèd time, that day, that hour,
 That warlike Locrine first did favour thee.   100
 Peace to the king of Brittany, my love,   [*Kneeling.*]
 Peace to all those that love and favour him.
Loc. (*taking her up.*) Doth Estrild fall with such
     submission
 Before her servant, king of Albion?
 Arise, fair lady; leave this lowly cheer;   105

101. *Kneeling.*] Hazlitt.

Lift up those looks that cherish Locrine's heart,
That I may freely view that roseal face
Which so entangled hath my lovesick breast.
Now to the court, where we will court it out,
And pass the night and day in Venus' sports.   110
Frolic, brave peers; be joyful with your king.

Exeunt.

SCENE III

Enter GUENDOLINE, THRASIMACHUS, MADAN *and the soldiers.*

Guen. You gentle winds, that with your modest blasts
    Pass through the circuit of the heavenly vault,
    Enter the clouds unto the throne of Jove,
    And bear my prayers to his all-hearing ears;
    For Locrine hath forsaken Guendoline,   5
    And learned to love proud Humber's concubine.
    You happy sprites, that in the concave sky
    With pleasant joy enjoy your sweetest love,
    Shed forth those tears with me which then you shed,
    When first you wooed your ladies to your wills;   10
    Those tears are fittest for my woeful case,
    Since Locrine shuns my nothing-pleasant face;
    Blush heavens, blush sun, and hide thy shining
        beams;
    Shadow thy radiant locks in gloomy clouds;
    Deny thy cheerful light unto the world,   15
    Where nothing reigns but falsehood and deceit.

V,iii,6. learned] *Simms*; learne *Q*; learnt *F*.

---

109. *court it out*] indulge in courting to the full.

V,iii,10. *wills*] desires.

13.] The appeal to the elements is a topic of the lament (Clemen, *English Tragedy*, p. 234).

SC. III]   TRAGEDY OF LOCRINE   125

>   What said I, falsehood? Ay, that filthy crime,
>   For Locrine hath forsaken Guendoline;
>   Behold the heavens do wail for Guendoline;
>   The shining sun doth blush for Guendoline;   20
>   The liquid air doth weep for Guendoline.
>   The very ground doth groan for Guendoline.
>   Ay, they are milder than the Briton king,
>   For he rejecteth luckless Guendoline.
> Thra. Sister, complaints are bootless in this cause; 25
>   This open wrong must have an open plague,
>   This plague must be repaid with grievous war,
>   This war must finish with Locrinus' death,
>   His death will soon extinguish our complaints.
> Guen. O no, his death will more augment my woes.   30
>   He was my husband, brave Thrasimachus,
>   More dear to me than the apple of mine eye;
>   Nor can I find in heart to work his scathe.
> Thra. Madam, if not your proper injuries
>   Nor my exile can move you to revenge,   35
>   Think on our father Corineus' words;
>   His words to us stands always for a law.
>   Should Locrine live that caused my father's death?
>   Should Locrine live that now divorceth you?
>   The heavens, the earth, the air, the fire reclaims, 40
>   And then why should all we deny the same?
> Guen. Then henceforth farewell womanish complaints,
>   All childish pity henceforth then farewell!
>   But cursèd Locrine, look unto thyself,
>   For Nemesis, the mistress of revenge,   45

  18-24.] "counterturn"; see note, IV,iii,15-20.
  25. *bootless*] void of boot or profit; hence, useless.
  25-29.] "marching figure," where a key word in one line becomes the subject of the next (Puttenham, *English Poesie*, Bk. III, chap. xix).
  32. *apple...eye*] proverbial; *Locrine* cited by Tilley, A290.
  33. *scathe*] "to do harm"; *Locrine* cited in the *O.E.D.* (*sb.*, 2.b).
  40. *reclaims*] say no; third person plural often ends in "s" (see Abbott, sec. 333).

                Sits armed at all points on our dismal blades;
                And cursèd Estrild, that inflamed his heart,
                Shall, if I live, die a reproachful death.
Madan. Mother, though nature makes me to lament
                My luckless father's froward lechery, 50
                Yet, for he wrongs my lady mother thus,
                I, if I could, myself would work his death.
Thra. See, madam, see, the desire of revenge
                Is in the children of a tender age.
                Forward, brave soldiers, into Mercia 55
                Where we shall brave the coward to his face. *Exeunt.*

SCENE IV

Enter LOCRINE, ESTRILD, SABREN, ASSARACUS *and the soldiers.*

Loc. Tell me, Assaracus, are the Cornish chuffs
                In such great number come to Mercia?
                And have they pitchèd there their petty host,
                So close unto our royal mansion?
Assar. They are, my lord, and mean incontinent 5
                To bid defiance to your majesty.
Loc. It makes me laugh to think that Guendoline
                Should have the heart to come in arms 'gainst me.

55. Mercia] *Rowe*; Mertia *Q.*

V,iv,0.1. SABREN] *Rowe*; Habren *Q*. 0.1. ASSARACUS] *Hazlitt*; Assarachus *Q*. 1. Assaracus] *Hazlitt*; Assarachus *Q*. 2. Mercia] *Rowe*; Mertia *Q*.

---

  48. *reproachful*] shameful.
  50. *froward*] bad or evilly disposed.

   V,iv,0.1. SABREN] here and at V,v,29.2 the 1595 quarto has "Habren," an alternative spelling of the name used by Holinshed (*Chronicles*, I,xiii); "Habren" is close to "Hafren" the Welsh name for the Severn (Tatlock, *Legendary History*, p. 29).
  1. *chuffs*] churls.
  5. *incontinent*] immediately.

SC. IV] TRAGEDY OF LOCRINE 127

Est. Alas, my lord, the horse will run amain
  When as the spur doth gall him to the bone; 10
  Jealousy, Locrine, hath a wicked sting.
Loc. Sayst thou so, Estrild, beauty's paragon?
  Well, we will try her choler to the proof,
  And make her know Locrine can brook no braves.
  March on, Assaracus; thou must lead the way, 15
  And bring us to their proud pavilion.   *Exeunt.*

SCENE V

Enter the Ghost *of* CORINEUS, *with thunder and lightning.*

Gho. Behold, the circuit of the azure sky
  Throws forth sad throbs, and grievous suspires,
  Prejudicating Locrine's overthrow;
  The fire casteth forth sharp darts of flames;
  The great foundation of the triple world 5
  Trembleth and quaketh with a mighty noise,
  Presaging bloody massacres at hand.
  The wandering birds that flutter in the dark
  When hellish Night, in cloudy chariot seated,
  Casteth her mists on shady Tellus' face, 10
  With sable mantles covering all the earth
  Now flies abroad amid the cheerful day,
  Foretelling some unwonted misery.

15. Assaracus] *Hazlitt*; Assarachus *Q.*

9-10. *horse...bone*] sounds proverbial; not recorded by Tilley.
14. *brook...braves*] not tolerate defiant threats.

V,v,2. *suspires*] obsolete word meaning sighs; *Locrine* cited by the *O.E.D.*
3. *Prejudicating*] presaging; *Locrine* cited by the *O.E.D.* (prejudicate, *v. Obs.*, 3).
5. *triple world*] Asia, Europe and Africa.
8. *birds*] probably refers to owls, birds of ill omen.
10. *Tellus*] the earth.

The snarling curs of darkened Tartarus,
Sent from Avernus' ponds by Rhadamanth, 15
With howling ditties pester every wood;
The watery ladies and the lightfoot fauns,
And all the rabble of the woody nymphs,
All trembling hide themselves in shady groves
And shroud themselves in hideous hollow pits. 20
The boisterous Boreas thundereth forth revenge;
The stony rocks cry out on sharp revenge;
The thorny bush pronounceth dire revenge.
                              Sound the alarm.
Now, Corineus, stay and see revenge,
And feed thy soul with Locrine's overthrow. 25
Behold, they come; the trumpets call them forth;
The roaring drums summon the soldiers;
Lo where their army glistereth on the plains.
Throw forth thy lightning, mighty Jupiter,
And pour thy plagues on cursèd Locrine's head! 30
                              Stand aside.

Enter LOCRINE, ESTRILD, ASSARACUS, SABREN *and their soldiers at one door;* THRASIMACHUS, GUENDOLINE, MADAN *and their followers at another.*

Loc. What, is the tiger started from his cave?
    Is Guendoline come from Cornubia,
    That thus she braveth Locrine to the teeth?
    And hast thou found thine armour, pretty boy,
    Accompanied with these thy straggling mates? 35
    Believe me, but this enterprise was bold,
    And well deserveth commendation.
Guen. Ay, Locrine, traitorous Locrine, we are come
    With full pretence to seek thine overthrow.

15. Rhadamanth] *Rowe*; Radamanth *Q*.   30.2. SABREN] *Rowe*; Habren *Q*.

17. *wat'ry ladies*] Naiads.
18. *woody nymphs*] Dryads.
33. *to...teeth*] directly and openly.
39. *pretence*] intention.

What have I done that thou shouldst scorn me thus? 40
What have I said that thou shouldst me reject?
Have I been disobedient to thy words?
Have I bewrayed thy arcane secrecy?
Have I dishonourèd thy marriage bed
With filthy crimes or with lascivious lusts? 45
Nay, it is thou that hast dishonoured it;
Thy filthy mind, o'ercome with filthy lusts,
Yieldeth unto affection's filthy darts.
Unkind, thou wrong'st thy first and truest fere;
Unkind, thou wrong'st thy best and dearest friend; 50
Unkind, thou scorn'st all skilful Brutus' laws,
Forgetting father, uncle, and thyself.

Est. Believe me, Locrine, but the girl is wise,
And well would seem to make a vestal nun,
How finely frames she her oration. 55

Thra. Locrine, we came not here to fight with words,
Words that can never win the victory.
But for you are so merry in your frumps,
Unsheath your swords and try it out by force,
That we may see who hath the better hand. 60

Loc. Think'st thou to dare me, bold Thrasimachus?
Think'st thou to fear me with thy taunting braves,
Or do we seem too weak to cope with thee?

54. vestal] *F*; vastall *Q*.

---

43. *bewrayed*] divulged.
43. *arcane*] secret; here a tautology.
48. *affection*] passion or feeling.
49-51.] example of "anaphora" or "report," where one word begins several lines in succession (Puttenham, *English Poesie*, Bk. III, chap. xix).
49. *fere*] companion in love.
56-60.] "The idea of pleading a cause with swords rather than words" was common; cf. *The Faerie Queene*, I,iv,42: "He neuer meant with words, but swords to plead his right" (Lyman, "Apocryphal Plays," *English Studies*, p. 219).
58. *frumps*] sneers (Steevens).
62. *fear me*] i.e., make me afraid.

Soon shall I show thee my fine cutting blade,
And with my sword, the messenger of death, 65
Seal thee an acquittance for thy bold attempts.

Exeunt.

[SCENE VI]

Sound the alarm. Enter LOCRINE, ASSARACUS *and a soldier at one door;* GUENDOLINE, THRASIMACHUS, *at another.* LOCRINE *and his followers driven back. Then let* LOCRINE *and* ESTRILD *enter again in a maze.*

Loc. O fair Estrilda, we have lost the field;
Thrasimachus hath won the victory,
And we are left to be a laughing-stock,
Scoffed at by those that are our enemies.
Ten thousand soldiers armed with sword and shield, 5
Prevail against an hundred thousand men.
Thrasimachus, incensed with fuming ire,
Rageth amongst the faint-heart soldiers
Like to grim Mars, when covered with his targe
He fought with Diomedes in the field, 10
Close by the banks of silver Simois.

Sound the alarm.

O, lovely Estrild, now the chase begins;
Ne'er shall we see the stately Troynovant
Mounted on the coursers garnished all with pearls;
Ne'er shall we view the fair Concordia, 15
Unless as captives we be thither brought.
Shall Locrine then be taken prisoner
By such a youngling as Thrasimachus?

V,vi. SCENE VI] *Simms.* 0.2. THRASIMACHUS] *F2*; Thrsimachus *Q*.
13. Troynovant] *F*; Traynouant *Q*.

---

66. *acquittance*] discharge or release; i.e., Thrasimachus will pay with his life for having insulted Locrine.

V,vi,0.4. *a maze*] state of bewilderment.
9-11.] see *Iliad*, V,837ff.

Shall Guendolina captivate my love?
Ne'er shall mine eyes behold that dismal hour; 20
Ne'er will I view that ruthful spectacle,
For with my sword, this sharp curtle-axe,
I'll cut in sunder my accursèd heart.
But O, you judges of the ninefold Styx,
Which with incessant torments rack the ghosts 25
Within the bottomless Abyssus' pits;
You gods, commanders of the heavenly spheres,
Whose will and laws irrevocable stands;
Forgive, forgive, this foul accursèd sin!
Forget, O gods, this foul condemnèd fault! 30
And now, my sword, that in so many fights
Kiss his sword.
Hast saved the life of Brutus and his son,
End now his life that wisheth still for death;
Work now his death that wisheth still for death;
Work now his death that hateth still his life. 35
Farewell, fair Estrild, beauty's paragon,
Framed in the front of forlorn miseries;
Ne'er shall mine eyes behold thy sunshine eyes,
But when we meet in the Elysian fields;
Thither I go before with hastened pace. 40
Farewell, vain world, and thy enticing snares.
Farewell, foul sin, and thy enticing pleasures.
And welcome, death, the end of mortal smart,
Welcome to Locrine's overburdened heart.
Thrust himself through with his sword.
Est. Break, heart, with sobs and grievous suspires, 45
Stream forth, you tears, from forth my watery eyes;
Help me to mourn for warlike Locrine's death;

40. hastened] *F*; hastenened *Q*. 42. Farewell] *F*; Forwell *Q*.

---

37. *in the front of*] to confront.
46-47.] self-apostrophe, a topic of the lament (Clemen, *English Tragedy*, p. 237).

            Pour down your tears, you watery regions,
            For mighty Locrine is bereft of life.
            O fickle Fortune! O unstable world!   50
            What else are all things that this globe contains,
            But a confusèd chaos of mishaps?
            Wherein, as in a glass, we plainly see,
            That all our life is but as a tragedy.
            Since mighty kings are subject to mishap--   55
            Ay, mighty kings are subject to mishap--
            Since martial Locrine is bereft of life,
            Shall Estrild live then after Locrine's death?
            Shall love of life bar her from Locrine's sword?
            O no, this sword, that hath bereft his life,   60
            Shall now deprive me of my fleeting soul;
            Strengthen these hands, O mighty Jupiter,
            That I may end my woeful misery.
            Locrine, I come; Locrine, I follow thee!

                                                         Kill herself.
                    Sound the alarm. Enter SABREN.
Sab.   What doleful sight, what rueful spectacle   65
            Hath Fortune offered to my hapless heart?
            My father slain with such a fatal sword,
            My mother murdered by a mortal wound!
            What Thracian dog, what barbarous Myrmidon,
            Would not relent at such a ruthful case?   70
            What fierce Achilles, what hard stony flint,
            Would not bemoan this mournful tragedy?
            Locrine, the map of magnanimity,
            Lies slaughtered in this foul accursèd cave;
            Estrild, the perfect pattern of renown,   75
            Nature's sole wonder, in whose beauteous breasts

50. Fortune] *F*; fortnne *Q*.   76. Nature's] *F*; Natnres *Q*.

   53-54.] see note III,i,16-17.
   55-56.] repetition; see Introduction, p. 15.
   73. *map*] "embodiment"; cf. *R2*, V,i,12: "Thou map of honour"
(Onions).

All heavenly grace and virtue was enshrined,
Both massacred, are dead within this cave;
And with them dies fair Pallas and sweet Love.
Here lies a sword, and Sabren hath a heart; 80
This blessèd sword shall cut my cursèd heart,
And bring my soul unto my parents' ghosts,
That they that live and view our tragedy,
May mourn our case with mournful plaudites.
      Let her offer to kill herself.
Ay me, my virgin's hands are too, too weak 85
To penetrate the bulwark of my breast;
My fingers, used to tune the amorous lute,
Are not of force to hold this steely glaive;
So I am left to wail my parents' death,
Not able for to work my proper death. 90
Ah, Locrine, honoured for thy nobleness,
Ah, Estrild, famous for thy constancy,
Ill may they fare that wrought your mortal ends!
          [Retires back.]

Enter GUENDOLINE, THRASIMACHUS, MADAN *and the soldiers.*

Guen. Search, soldiers, search; find Locrine and his
   love;
Find the proud strumpet, Humber's concubine, 95
That I may change those her so pleasing looks,
To pale and ignominious aspèct.
Find me the issue of their cursèd love;
Find me young Sabren, Locrine's only joy,
That I may glut my mind with lukewarm blood, 100
Swiftly distilling from the bastard's breast.

88. glaive] *Rowe*; glaine *Q*. 89. left] *F*; lieft *Q*. 93.1. *Retires back.*] *Moltke.*

---

79. *Pallas*] goddess of wisdom.
84. *plaudites*] applause; the rhythm requires three syllables.
88. *glaive*] spear.
92. *constancy*] The expected lament seems to overwhelm the author's sense of the situation; Estrild has not proven to be a model of constancy.
101. *distilling*] trickling down.

| | TRAGEDY OF LOCRINE | [ACT V |

    My father's ghost still haunts me for revenge,
    Crying, "Revenge my over-hastened death."
    My brother's exile and mine own divorce,
    Banish remorse clean from my brazen heart,   105
    All mercy from mine adamantine breasts.
Thra. Nor doth thy husband, lovely Guendoline,
    That wonted was to guide our stayless steps,
    Enjoy this light; see where he murdered lies
    By luckless lot and froward frowning fate;   110
    And by him lies his lovely paramour,
    Fair Estrild, gorèd with a dismal sword
    And, as it seems, both murdered by themselves,
    Clasping each other in their feebled arms
    With loving zeal, as if for company   115
    Their uncontented corpse were yet content
    To pass foul Styx in Charon's ferry-boat.
Guen. And hath proud Estrild then prevented me?
    Hath she escapèd Guendolina's wrath
    Violently by cutting off her life?   120
    Would God she had the monstrous Hydra's lives,
    That every hour she might have died a death
    Worse than the swing of old Ixion's wheel;
    And every hour revive to die again,
    As Tityus, bound to houseless Caucasus,   125

---

106. adamantine] *Rowe;* adamintive *Q.*   125. Caucasus] *Hazlitt;* Caucason *Q.*

---

    108. *stayless*] "ever-moving, unceasing" (*O.E.D.*, a.^{1}, 1).
    110. *froward*] adverse.
    116. *corpse*] until 1750, the singular and plural usually had the same spelling, "corps," although "corpses" was occasionally used (*O.E.D.*); the modern plural "corpses" would disrupt the metre.
    118. *prevented*] deprived of "a purpose, expectation," i.e., the pleasure of taking vengeance on Estrild (*O.E.D.*, prevent, v., 6).
    120. *Violently by*] normal order inverted for emphasis.
    125-128. *Tityus...die*] Because he assaulted Leto, Tityus was punished in Hades by having two vultures tear at his liver (*O.C.D.*). The dramatist may be confusing Tityus with Prometheus, who suffered a similar punishment but was chained to a mountain in the Caucasus range. Prometheus was immortal and, thus, each night his liver grew whole again so that he could be punished the following day. The "want of food" seems to be a secondary affliction.

SC. VI]   TRAGEDY OF LOCRINE   135

   Doth feed the substance of his own mishap
   And every day for want of food doth die,
   And every night doth live, again to die.
   But stay, methinks I hear some fainting voice
   Mournfully weeping for their luckless death. 130
Sab. [coming forward.] You mountain nymphs, which in
    these deserts reign,
   Cease off your hasty chase of savage beasts;
   Prepare to see a heart oppressed with care;
   Address your ears to hear a mournful style.
   No human strength, no work can work my weal, 135
   Care in my heart so tyrant-like doth deal.
   You Dryades and lightfoot Satyri,
   You gracious fairies, which at evening tide
   Your closets leave with heavenly beauty stored,
   And on your shoulders spread your golden locks; 140
   You savage bears in caves and darkened dens,
   Come wail with me the martial Locrine's death;
   Come mourn with me for beauteous Estrild's death.
   Ah, loving parents, little do you know
   What sorrow Sabren suffers for your thrall. 145
Guen. But may this be, and is it possible?
   Lives Sabren yet to expiate my wrath?
   Fortune, I thank thee for this courtesy;
   And let me never see one prosperous hour,
   If Sabren die not a reproachful death. 150
Sab. Hard-hearted Death, that when the wretched call
   Art furthest off and seldom hear'st at all;
   But in the midst of Fortune's good success
   Uncallèd comes, and shears our life in twain;

131. *coming forward.*] *This ed.* 138. gracious] *F*; gtacious *Q*.
141. savage] *Rowe*; saпadge *Q*.

 137. *Satyri*] Satyrs, half-goat and half-man.
 139. *closets*] secret places, retreats.
 142-143.] "lugete-topos" where the mourner calls on others to assist in his lamentation (Clemen, *English Tragedy*, pp. 232-33).

When will that hour, that blessèd hour, draw nigh, 155
When poor distressèd Sabren may be gone?
Sweet Atropos, cut off my fatal thread!
What art thou, Death? shall not poor Sabren die?

Guen. (*taking her by the chin shall say thus*) Yes,
    damsel, yes, Sabren shall surely die,
Though all the world should seek to save her life; 160
And not a common death shall Sabren die,
But after strange and grievous punishments
Shortly inflicted upon thy bastard's head,
Thou shalt be cast into the cursèd streams,
And feed the fishes with thy tender flesh.   165

Sab. And think'st thou then, thou cruel homicide,
That these thy deeds shall be unpunishèd?
No, traitor, no; the gods will 'venge these wrongs,
The fiends of hell will mark these injuries.
Never shall these blood-sucking masty curs   170
Bring wretched Sabren to her latest home,
For I myself, in spite of thee and thine,
Mean to abridge my former destinies,
And that which Locrine's sword could not perform,
This pleasant stream shall present bring to pass. 175
                              She drowneth herself.

Guen. One mischief follows on another's neck;
Who would have thought so young a maid as she
With such a courage would have sought her death?
And for because this river was the place

166. think'st] *F*; thinst *Q*.   176. on] *Rowe*; *not in Q*.

---

170. *masty*] "burly"; obsolete form of "mastiff" (*O.E.D.*, a., 3).
176.] This proverbial expression, cited by Tilley (M1004, "Mischiefs, like waves, never come alone"), also appears in Wilmot, *Tancred and Gismund*, 1.1851: "One mischiefe brings another on his neck"; the printed version of Wilmot's play contains a commendatory letter dated August 8, 1591, but we cannot assume that *Locrine* borrows the line from *Tancred and Gismund* because there is the possibility that a manuscript version of *Locrine* was available to Wilmot.

SC. VI] TRAGEDY OF LOCRINE 137

    Where little Sabren resolutely died, 180
    Sabren forever shall this same be called.
    And as for Locrine, our deceasèd spouse,
    Because he was the son of mighty Brute,
    To whom we owe our country, lives and goods,
    He shall be buried in a stately tomb, 185
    Close by his agèd father Brutus' bones,
    With such great pomp and great solemnity,
    As well beseems so brave a prince as he.
    Let Estrild lie without the shallow vaults,
    Without the honour due unto the dead, 190
    Because she was the author of this war.
    Retire, brave followers, unto Troynovant,
    Where we will celebrate these exequies,
    And place young Locrine in his father's tomb.
                           Exeunt omnes.
             [*Enter* ATE.]

Ate. Lo! here the end of lawless treachery, 195
    Of usurpation and ambitious pride;
    And they that for their private amours dare
    Turmoil our land, and set their broils abroach,
    Let them be warnèd by these premises.
    And as a woman was the only cause 200
    That civil discord was then stirrèd up,
    So let us pray for that renownèd maid,
    That eight and thirty years the sceptre swayed
    In quiet peace and sweet felicity;
    And every wight that seeks her grace's smart, 205
    Would that this sword were piercèd in his heart.
                                  Exit.
              FINIS.

189. vaults] *F*; vauts *Q*. 194.2. *Enter* ATE.] *M*. 198. set] *F*; see *Q*. 206. Would] *F*; Wold *Q*.

---

198. *abroach*] astir.
199. *premises*] things that have happened before.
203.] see Introduction, pp. 4-5.

APPENDIX A

THE MIRROR FOR MAGISTRATES: "ALBANACT," 11.414-518

(See Introduction, p. 2)

"No marueyle sure though you, herewith be sad,
"You noble *Britaynes*, for your *Brutus* sake:
"Sithe whilome me your captaine stout you had,
"That nowe my leaue and last farewell must take:
"Thus nature willes me once an ende to make:
"And leaue you here behinde, which after mee:
"Shall come as I departe before you see.

"You wot wherfore I with the *Grecians* foughte,
"With dinte of sworde I made their force to flye:
"*Antenors* frendes on *Tuscane* shores I soughte,
"And did you not my promiste lande denye.
"By *Martiall* powre I made the *Frenchemen* flye,
"Where you to saue I loste my faithfull frende:
"For you, at *Tours* my *Turnus* tooke his ende.

"I nede not now, resite what loue I bare,
"My frendship you I truste haue founde so well:
"That none emongste you all which present are,
"With teares doth not recorde the tale I tell.
"Eke whom I founde for vertues to excell,
"To them I gaue the price therof as dewe:
"As they deserude, whose factes I founde so true.

"Nowe must I proue, if paynes were well bestowde,
"Or if I spente my gratefull giftes in vayne:
"Or if these great good turnes to you I owde,
"And might not aske your loyall loues agayne.
"Which if I wist what tonge could tell my payne,
"I meane if you vngratefull mindes do beare:
"What meaneth death, to let me linger here.

"For if you shall abuse your prince in this,
"The Goddes on you for such an heynous facte:
"To take reuenge be sure will neuer misse:
"And then to late you will repente the acte,
"When all my realme and all your welthes are sacte,
"But if you shall as you begon procede:
"Of kingdomes fall or foes there is no dreede.

"And to auoyde contention that may fall,
"Because I wishe this realme the *Britaynes* still:
"Therfore I will declare before you all,
"Sithe you are come, my whole intent and will.
"Which if you kepe, and wreste it not to ill,
"There is no doubt, but euermore with fame:
"You shall enioye the *Britaynes* realme and name.

"You see my sonnes, that after me must raigne,
"Whom you or this haue liekte and counsaylde well:
"You know what erst you wisht they should refraine,
"Which way they might all vices vile expell:
"Which way they might in vertues great excell:
"Thus if you shall, when I am gone insue,
"You shall discharge the truste reposde in you.

"Be you their fathers, with your counsayle wise,
"And you my children take them euen as mee.
"Be you their guydes, in what you can deuise:
"And let their good instructions teache you three,
"Be faithful all, as brethren ought agree:
"For concorde kepes a realme, in stable staye:
"But discorde bringes all kingdomes to decaye.

"Recorde to this mine eldest sonne I giue,
"This midle parte of realme to holde his owne:
"And to his heyres that after him shall lyue,
"Also to *Camber* that his parte be knowne,
"I giue that lande that lies welnighe oregrowne:
"With woodes Norwest & mountaynes mighty hie,
"Twene this and that, the *Stutiae* stream doth lye.

"And vnto the my yongest sonne that arte,
"Myne *Albanacte* I giue to thee likewise:
"As muche to be for thee and thine a parte,
"As Northe beyonde the arme of sea there lyes.
"Of which loe here, a map before your eyes,
"Lo here my sonnes my kingdome all you haue:
"For which I nought, but this remember craue.

"Firste that you take these fathers graue for mee,
"Imbrace their counsaile euen as it were myne:
"Next that betwene your selues you will agree,
"And neuer one at others welthe repine:
"See that ye byde still bounde with frendly lyne,
"And laste my subiectes, with such loue retayne:
"As long they may your subiectes eke remayne.

"Lo nowe I fele my breath beginnes to fayle,
"My time is come, giue eche to me your hande,
"Farewell, farewell, to mourne will not preuayle:
"I see with knife where *Atropos* doth stande,
"Farewell my frendes, my children and my lande,
"And farewell all my subiectes, farewell breathe,
"Farewell ten thousand tymes, and welcome deathe.

And euen with that he turnde, himselfe a syde,
And gasped thryse, ˙and gaue away the ghost:
Then all at once with mourning voyce they cryde.
And all his subiects eke, from lest to most
Lamenting fild with wayling teares ech coast:
Perdy the *Britaynes* all, with one assent:
Did for their king, full doulfully lament.

But what auayles, to striue against the tyde?
Or els to sayle, against the streame and winde:
What booteth it against the clyues to ryde:
Or els to worke against the course of kinde?
Sith nature hath the ende of thinges assinde,
There is no nay, we must perforce departe:
Gainst dint of death, there is no ease by arte.

As custome wild wee funerals preparde,
And al with mourning cloathes, and chere did come:
To laye this king on Beere we had regarde,
In Royal sort, as did his corps become,
His Herce prepard, we brought him to his tombe,
At *Troynouant*, he built where he did dye,
Was he entombde: his Royal corps doth lye.

APPENDIX B

THE COMPLAINT OF ELSTRED, 11.181-222, 409-432

(See Introduction, p. 3)

For where I lost my loue, my friends, my hope,
There found I hope, there faithful friends, there loue:
And whilst I went fast fettered in a rope,
Weeping such teares as might compassion moue,
    I was presented by vnhallowed hand,
    To stoute *Locrinus* King of *Logiers* land.

Who like that thunder-threatning Potentate,
The Arbiter of changes and increase,
Sate lightning forth such lookes as might amate
Warre-breeding *Mars*, the countercheck of peace:
    Him when I saw, I shooke, and shaking wept,
    And weeping, to his throne for mercy crept.

And whilst I rent my carelesse-scattered locks,
Those tricked trammels where true loue was tangled,
At *Locrins* breast for mercy fancie knocks,
Shadowed in seemely lookes where-with loue angled:
    And when I cry'd, O pitty me my King,
    His eyes cry'd pitty me, by woe looking.

Each motion of mine eyes, enforc't commotion
Betwixt his will and reason what to aunswere:
(But will where loue will rule, must haue promotion.)
My sute first past for life, with listning eare
    He heard, and graunted what I did require,
    Ennobling of my life by his desire.

My bonds newe broke, and I from fetters los'd,
As mount the brother twinnes from waterie vast,
Within fayre *Thetis* liquid lappe fore-clos'd,
So from their humbled closures lightned fast
    My louely lampes, which earst made intercession,
    And by one looke, of all harts tooke possession.

All wonder, and with dazeled eyes with-draw them,
Onely the right-borne Egle by these lights
Approu'd his birth-right, and no sooner saw them
Apparailed in hope, and choyce delights,
    But vp he lookes, by suddaine sight confounded,
    And I by selfe-like sight, was likely wounded.

"For where there growes a simpathie of harts,
"Each passion in the one, the other paineth,
"And by each cariage of the outward parts,
(Wherein the actuall worke of loue remaineth)
    The inward griefes, mislikes, and ioyes are tought:
    And euery signe bewraies a secrete thought.

409-432,

Sweet Image of his lyuing excellence,
Whilst thus it lay (ah-las that thus it lay)
Impatient greefe would leaue me no defence,
I cald on death, but teares wept death away.
    His worst was past, I sigh'd, but sighes nor slender
    Teares worke no truce, but where the hart is tender.

And as the straw vnto the Iette fast cleaueth,
So clunge I both myne armes about his necke:
Pouring my plaints in eares that nought conceaueth.
Ah loue (quoth I) vnkind, why dost thou checke,
    Why dost thou mate the minds that most admire thee,
    And in our needes, inconstant thus retire thee?

Breathe life in him againe, or leaue me breathlesse,
Or from thine enuious tryumphant throne,
Send forth *Despayre* with locks vnkempt and wreathlesse,
To ioyne by death two soules in life but one.
    And since at once our harts thou didst inspire,
    Let both of vs (O Loue) at once expire.

Oh spent on barraine ground, my flood-like weeping
Loue would not heare: tho gan I trembling try
If kisses could reuiue his ceaslesse sleeping,
But death repines these baites of fond desire.
    I suckt his wounds, and wrapt them round about,
    But (ah) the life before was issued out.

APPENDIX C

COMPARISON OF *SELIMUS* (11.414-416, 2422-2429), *LOCRINE* (II,vi,1-17), AND "RUINES OF ROME" (11.149-166)

(See Introduction, p. 8)

Selimus, 11.414-416, 2422-2429,

1. If *Selimus* were once your Emperour,
2. Ide dart abroad the thunderbolts of warre,
3. And mow their hartlesse squadrons to the ground.

4. Were they as mightie and as fell of force,
5. As those old earth-bred brethren, which once
6. Heape hill on hill to scale the starrie skie,
7. When *Briareus* arm'd with a hundreth hands,
8. Flung foorth a hundreth mountaines at great *Ioue*,
9. And when the monstrous giant *Monichus*
10. Hurld mount Olimpus at great *Mars* his targe,
11. And darted cedars at Mineruas shield.

Locrine, II,vi,1-17,

1. How bravely this young Briton, Albanact,
2. Darteth abroad the thunderbolts of war,
3. Beating down millions with his furious mood,
4. And in his glory triumphs over all;
5. Moving the massy squadrants of the ground,
6. Heap hills on hills, to scale the starry sky,
7. As when Briareus, armed with an hundred hands,
8. Flung forth an hundred mountains at great Jove,
9. And when the monstrous giant, Monichus,
10. Hurled Mount Olympus at great Mars his targe,
11. And shot huge cedars at Minerva's shield.
12. How doth he overlook with haughty front
13. My fleeting hosts, and lifts his lofty face
14. Against us all that now do fear his force;
15. Like as we see the wrathful sea from far,
16. In a great mountain heaped, with hideous noise,
17. With thousand billows beat against the ships.

"Ruines of Rome," ll.149-166,

1. Then gan that Nation, th'earths new Giant brood,
2. To dart abroad the thunder bolts of warre,
3. And beating downe these walls with furious mood
4. Into her mothers bosome, all did marre;
5. To th'end that none, all were it *Ioue* his sire
6. Should boast himselfe of the Roman Empire.

7. Like as whilome the children of the earth
8. Heapt hils on hils, to scale the starrie skie,
9. And fight against the Gods of heauenly berth,
10. Whiles *Ioue* at them his thunderbolts let flie;
11. All suddenly with lightning ouerthrowne,
12. The furious squadrons downe to ground did fall,
13. That th'earth vnder her childrens weight did grone,
14. And th'heauens in glorie triumpht ouer all:
15. So did that haughtie front which heaped was
16. On these seuen Romane hils, it selfe vpreare
17. Ouer the world, and lift her loftie face
18. Against the heauen, that gan her force to feare.

An examination of the borrowed passages in the plays indicates that *Locrine* originally borrowed from Spenser and that *Selimus*, in turn, borrowed from *Locrine*. *Locrine* borrowed more extensively from the *Complaints*, generally, and from the "Ruines of Rome": lines 3 and 4 in *Locrine* are adapted from "Ruines" lines 3 and 14; similarly, *Locrine*, lines 12-14 are derived from lines 15-18 of the "Ruines." The borrowings from the "Ruines of Rome" in *Locrine* are not limited to the lines quoted above: *Locrine*, lines 15-17, are borrowed from lines 211-13 in the "Ruines"--

Like as ye see the wrathfull Sea from farre,
In a great mountaine heap't with hideous noyse,
Eftsoones of thousand billowes shouldred narre;

the last speech of Brutus also takes lines from the "Ruines." The fact that *Locrine* borrows extensively from the "Ruines" and the borrowings in *Selimus* are limited to those found in *Locrine* suggests that *Locrine* is the original borrower. Lines 6-11 in both plays are in complete agreement except that line 7 in *Locrine* has been emended to read "As when," and in the last line, 11, *Selimus* reads "darted" where *Locrine* has "shot huge"; both plays have the reading "Heap" whereas the past tense would seem to require the Spenserian word, "Heapt."[1] *Locrine* retains the reading "hills on hills" found in Spenser while *Selimus* has "hill on hill." In two cases, however, *Selimus* is closer to the Spenserian original. The line in *Selimus*, "As those old earth-bred brethren, which once," adapted from Spenser's line, "Which whilom did those earthborn brethren blinde" (140), appears to have been omitted in *Locrine* after "Moving the massy squadrants of the ground," and the omission is evident because the sense is marred.[2] The line immediately preceding this apparent omission, "Moving the massy squadrants of the ground," poses another difficulty because the corresponding line in *Selimus*, "And mow their hartlesse squadrons to the ground," preserves the sense and words from the Spenserian line "The furious squadrons downe to ground did fall" whereas *Locrine* has altered the idea and introduced the unusual word "squadrants." Baldwin suggests that the compositor had difficulty with this line because the acting version of *Locrine* was marked badly, resulting in the omission of one line and the faulty printing of the line immediately preceding.[3] If, indeed, the compositor of *Locrine* has faithfully followed his copy, then the question arises concerning the origin of the corresponding line in *Selimus*; the only possible answer is that the author of *Selimus* consulted Spenser independently for the line "And now their hartlesse squadrons to the ground."

Notes To Appendix C

[1]Baldwin discusses this error in *Literary Genetics*, p. 222.
[2]Kenneth Muir, "'Locrine' and 'Selimus'," *Times Literary Supplement*, August 12, 1944, p. 391.
[3]*Literary Genetics*, p. 222.

BIBLIOGRAPHY

PRIMARY WORKS

Camden, William. *Camden's Britannia, 1695*. A Facsimile of the 1695 edition published by Edmund Gibson [translated from the Latin] with an introduction by Stuart Piggott and a bibliographical note by Gwyn Walters. Newton Abbot, Devon: David and Charles Reprints, 1971.

Cooper, Thomas. *Thesaurus Linguae Romanae et Britannicae 1565*. Facsimile reprint of 1565 edition. Menston, England: The Scolar Press, 1969.

Davenport, Robert. *King John and Matilda*. In *Elizabethan History Plays*, edited with an introduction and glossary by William A. Armstrong. London: Oxford University Press, 1965.

Edward the Third. In *Elizabethan History Plays*, edited with an introduction and glossary by William A. Armstrong. London: Oxford University Press, 1965.

Elyot, Sir Thomas. *The Book Named the Governor*. Edited with an introduction by S.E. Lehmberg. London: Dent, 1962.

Fabyan, Robert. *The Great Chronicle of London*. Edited by A.H. Thomas...and J.D. Thornley. London: C.W. Jones, 1938.

Famous Victories of Henry the Fifth, The. In *Chief Pre-Shakespearean Dramas*, edited by Joseph Quincy Adams. Cambridge, Massachusetts: Houghton Mifflin, 1924.

Geoffrey of Monmouth. *Histories of the Kings of Britain*. Translated by Sebastian Evans. London: Dent, 1912.

Grafton, Richard. *Grafton's Chronicle; or, History of England...* 2 vols. London: J. Johnson [etc.], 1809.

Greene, Robert. *The Plays and Poems of Robert Greene*. Edited with introductions and notes by J. Churton Collins. 2 vols. Oxford: Clarendon Press, 1905.

Greene, Robert. *The Scottish History of James the Fourth*. Edited by Norman Sanders. London: Methuen, 1970.

Greg, Walter W., ed. *Two Elizabethan Stage Abridgements: The Battle of Alcazar & Orlando Furioso*. Oxford: Oxford University Press, for the Malone Society, 1923.

Grosart, Alexander B., ed. *The Life and Complete Works in Prose and Verse of Robert Greene, M.A.* 15 vols. (Reissue of London edition, 1881-86). New York: Russell & Russell, 1964.

Hardyng, John. *The Chronicle of John Hardyng containing an account of Public Transactions from the earliest period of English History to the Beginning of the Reign of King Edward the Fourth. Together with the Continuation by Richard Grafton, to the thirty fourth year of King Henry the Eighth*. To which are added a Biographical and Literary Preface and an Index by Henry Ellis. London, 1812.

Henslowe's Diary, Part I Text. Edited by Walter W. Greg. London: A.H. Bullen, 1904.

_____, *Part II, Commentary*. Edited by Walter W. Greg. London: A.H. Bullen, 1908.

Holinshed, Raphael. *The first and second [and third] volumes of chronicles...first collected and published by Raphaell Holinshed, William Harrison, and others: now newlie augmented and continued...to...1586, by Iohn Hooker...and others...*[London, 1587]. (Ann Arbor, Michigan: University Microfilms. Original now in Huntington Library.)

Homer. *The Iliad*. Translated by Robert Fitzgerald. Garden City, New York: Anchor Press/Doubleday, 1974.

Hughes, Thomas. *The Misfortunes of Arthur*. In *Early English Classical Tragedies*, edited with introduction and notes by John W. Cunliffe. Oxford: Clarendon Press, 1912.

Interlude of Vice, The (Horestes) 1567. Edited by Daniel Seltzer. Oxford: Oxford University Press, for the Malone Society, 1962.

Knack to Know a Knave, A. Edited by G.R. Proudfoot. Oxford: Oxford University Press, for the Malone Society, 1963.

Kyd, Thomas. *The Spanish Tragedy*. Edited by Philip Edwards. London: Methuen, 1959.

Lamentable Tragedy of Locrine, The. London: Thomas Creede, 1595.

Lodge, Thomas and Robert Greene. *A Looking Glasse for London and England*. Edited by Tetsumaro Hayashi. Metuchen, N.J.: Scarecrow Press, 1970.

Lodge, Thomas. *The Complaint of Elstred.* In vol. 2 (59-84) of *The Complete Works of Thomas Lodge, 1580-1623?* New York: Russell & Russell, 1963.

_____. *The Wounds of Civil War.* Edited by Joseph W. Houppert. Lincoln: University of Nebraska Press, 1969.

Marlowe, Christopher. *Dido, Queen of Carthage, and The Massacre at Paris.* Edited by H.J. Oliver. Cambridge, Massachusetts: Harvard University Press, 1968.

_____. *Tamburlaine the Great, Parts I & II.* Edited by Tatiana A. Wolff. London: Methuen, 1964.

Milton, John. *The History of Britain.* In vol. 10 (1-325) of *The Works of John Milton*, edited by George Philip Krapp. New York: Columbia University Press, 1932.

Mirror for Magistrates, The. Parts added by John Higgins and Thomas Blenerhasset. Edited from the original texts in the Huntington Library by Lily B. Campbell. Cambridge: Cambridge University Press, 1946.

Norton, Thomas and Thomas Sackville. *Gorboduc.* In *Five Elizabethan Tragedies*, edited with an introduction by A.K. McIlwraith. London: Oxford University Press, 1938.

Ovid. *Ovid's Heroïdes, Amours, Art of Love, Remedy of Love and Minor Works.* Translated by Henry T. Riley. Vol. 3 of the Classical Library translation of the works of Ovid. London: G. Bell and Sons, 1910.

_____. *The Metamorphoses.* Translated by Horace Gregory. New York: New American Library of World Literature, 1960.

Peele, George. *The Life and Works of George Peele.* General Editor, Charles Tyler Prouty. 3 vols. New Haven: Yale University Press, 1952-1970.

Pettie, George. *A Petite Pallace of Pettie His Pleasure.* Edited by I. Gallancz. 2 vols. London: Chatto & Windus, 1908.

Preston, Thomas. *A Lamentable Tragedie Mixed Full of Plesant Mirth, Containing the Life of Cambises, King of Percia.* In *Chief Pre-Shakespearean Dramas*, edited by Joseph Quincy Adams. Cambridge, Massachusetts: Houghton Mifflin, 1924.

Puttenham, George. *The Arte of English Poesie.* Edited by Gladys Doidge Willcock and Alice Walker. Cambridge: Cambridge University Press, 1936.

Rastell, John. *The Cronycles of Englande and of dyvers other realmes* ... London? 153-. (Ann Arbor, Michigan: University Microfilms. Original now in Huntington Library.)

Seneca. *His Tenne Tragedies Translated into English.* Edited by Thomas Newton Anno 1581. With an introduction by T.S. Eliot. 2 vols. London: Constable, 1927.

Shakespeare, William. *The Doubtful Plays of Shakespeare.* Edited by Henry Tyrrell. London, 1851.

_____. *Doubtful Plays of Wm. Shakespeare.* Edited by Max Moltke. Leipzig, 1869.

_____. *Mr. William Shakespeare's Comedies, Histories and Tragedies.* Reproduced in facsimile from the edition of 1664. London: Methuen, 1905.

_____. *Mr. William Shakespeare's Comedies, Histories and Tragedies.* Reproduced in facsimile from the edition of 1685. London: Methuen, 1904.

_____. *The Poems.* Edited by F.T. Prince. London: Methuen, 1960.

_____. *Supplement to the Edition of Shakespear's Plays Published in 1778 by S. Johnson and G. Steevens...With Notes by the Editor and Others.* Edited by Edmund Malone. 2 vols. London, 1780.

_____. *A Supplement to the Plays.* Edited by W.G. Simms. New York, 1848.

_____. *The Supplementary Works of William Shakspeare.* Edited by William Hazlitt. London, 1852.

_____. *The Works of Mr. William Shakspear.* Edited by Nicholas Rowe. 6 vols. London, 1709.

_____. *The Works of Shakespear.* Edited by Alexander Pope. 9 vols. London, 1728.

Six Old English Chronicles. Edited by J.A. Giles. London: George Bell & Sons, 1891.

Spenser, Edmund. *Poetical Works.* Edited with critical notes by J.C. Smith and E. De Selincourt, with an introduction by E. De Selincourt and a glossary. London: Oxford University Press, 1912.

Stow, John. *The annales of England, from the first inhabitation vntill 1592. Continued unto 1631. (An appendix, etc. 1632).* 2 parts. London: printed by A.M[athewes] for R. Meighen, 1631, 32. (Ann Arbor, Michigan: University Microfilms.)

Swinburne, Algernon Charles. *Locrine.* In vol. 4 (137-239) of *Complete Works*, edited by Sir Edmund Gosse and Thomas James Wise. London: W. Heinemann, 1926.

Tragedy of Locrine 1595, The. Edited by Ronald B. McKerrow. Oxford: Oxford University Press, for the Malone Society, 1908.

Tragedy of Tancred and Gismund 1591-2, The. Edited by W.W. Greg. Oxford: Oxford University Press, for the Malone Society, 1914.

Tragical Reign of Selimus, The. Edited by W. Bang. London: Charles Whittingham, for the Malone Society, 1908.

Transcript of the Registers of the Company of Stationers of London 1554-1640 A.D. Edited by Edward Arber. 5 vols. London: Privately Printed, 1875-1877. Vol. 5 printed privately in Birmingham, 1894.

Vergil, Polydore. *Historia Anglica*. A Scolar Press Facsimile of 1555 edition (Basilea). Menston, England: The Scolar Press, 1972.

Weakest Goeth to the Wall 1600, The. Edited by W.W. Greg. Oxford: Oxford University Press, for the Malone Society, 1912.

Whitney, Geffrey. *A Choice of Emblemes*. Edited by Henry Green with an introduction by Frank Fieler. New York: B. Blom, 1967.

SECONDARY WORKS

Abbott, E.A. *A Shakespearian Grammar*. Reprinted from the 1870 edition of Macmillan and Company. New York: Dover Publications, 1966.

Acheson, Arthur. *Shakespeare, Chapman and Sir Thomas More*. New York: E.B. Hackett, 1931.

Adams, Joseph Quincy. "Hill's List of Early Plays in Manuscript," *Library*, 4th ser., 20 (1940), 71-99.

Anglo, Sydney. "The British History in Early Tudor Propaganda," *Bulletin of the John Rylands Library*, 44 (1961), 17-48.

Armstrong, William A. "The Elizabethan Concept of the Tyrant," *Review of English Studies*, 22 (1946), 161-181.

Ashley, Leonard R.N. *Authorship and Evidence*. Genève: Librairie Droz, 1968.

Baker, Howard. *Induction to Tragedy: A Study in a Development of Form in Gorboduc, The Spanish Tragedy, and Titus Andronicus*. New York: Russell & Russell, 1965.

Bald, R.C. "The *Locrine* and *George-A-Greene* Title-Page Inscriptions," *Library*, 4th ser., 15 (1935), 295-305.

Baldwin, Thomas Whitfield. *On the Literary Genetics of Shakspere's Plays 1592-1594*. Urbana: University of Illinois Press, 1959.

Barish, Jonas. "The Spanish Tragedy, or the Pleasures and Perils of Rhetoric," *Elizabethan Theatre, Stratford-Upon-Avon Studies*, 9 (1966), 59-85.

Baskervill, C.R. *The Elizabethan Jig and Related Song Drama.* Chicago: University of Chicago Press, 1929.

Bennett, Josephine W. *The Evolution of "The Faerie Queene."* Chicago: University of Chicago Press, 1942.

Bentley, G.E. "Authenticity and Attribution in the Jacobean and Caroline Drama," *English Institute Annual*, 1942, pp. 101-118.

Bethell, Samuel L. "The Comic Element in Shakespeare's Histories," *Anglia*, 71 (1952), 82-101.

Bevington, David. *Tudor Drama and Politics.* Cambridge, Massachusetts: Harvard University Press, 1968.

Boas, Frederick S. *An Introduction to Tudor Drama.* Oxford: Clarendon Press, 1933.

Böhm, Rudolf. *Wesen und Funktion der Sterberede im elisabethanischen Drama.* No. 13 of *Britannica et Americana.* Hamburg: Cram, de Gruyter, 1964.

Bowers, Fredson. *Bibliography and Textual Criticism.* Oxford: Clarendon Press, 1964.

_____. "Elizabethan Proofing," *Joseph Quincy Adams Memorial Studies*, ed. James G. McManaway, Giles E. Dawson and Edwin E. Willoughby. Washington: The Folger Shakespeare Library, 1948.

_____. *Elizabethan Revenge Tragedy 1587-1642.* Princeton: Princeton University Press, 1940.

_____. "Notes on Running-Titles as Bibliographical Evidence," *Library*, 4th ser., 19 (1938-39), 315-338.

_____. *On Editing Shakespeare.* Charlottesville: University Press of Virginia, 1966.

Bradbrook, Muriel C. *Elizabethan Stage Conditions.* Hamden, Conn.: Archon Books, 1962.

_____. "Shakespeare and his Collaborators," *Shakespeare 1971*, ed. Clifford Leech and J.M.R. Margeson. Toronto: University of Toronto Press, 1972.

_____. *Themes and Conventions of Elizabethan Tragedy.* Cambridge: Cambridge University Press, 1935.

Braginton, Mary V. "Two Notes on Senecan Tragedy," *Modern Language Notes*, 41 (1926), 468-469.

Braun, Margareta. *Symbolişmus und Illusionismus im englischen Drama vor 1620.* München: Universität zu München, 1962.

Bridges-Adams, William. *The Irresistible Theatre.* London: Secker & Warburg, 1957.

Briggs, Katharine M. *The Anatomy of Puck; an Examination of Fairy Beliefs among Shakespeare's Contemporaries and Successors.* London: Routledge and Kegan Paul, 1959.

Briggs, William Dinsmore, ed. *Marlowe's Edward ii.* London: David Nutt, 1914.

Brooke, C.F. Tucker. "The Marlowe Canon," *Publications of the Modern Language Association,* 37 (1922), 367-417.

_____, ed. *The Shakespeare Apocrypha.* Oxford: Clarendon Press, 1908.

_____. *The Tudor Drama.* Boston: Houghton Mifflin, 1911.

Brooks, Alden. *Will Shakespeare and the Dyer's Hand.* New York: Scribner, 1943.

Brotanek, Rudolf. "Plagiate im *Locrine,*" *Beiblatt zur Anglia,* 23 (1900), 202-207.

Burford, Albert H. "History and Biography: the Renaissance Distinction," *A Tribute to George Coffin Taylor,* ed. Arnold Williams. Chapel Hill: University of North Carolina Press, 1952.

Buland, Mable. *The Presentation of Time in the Elizabethan Drama.* Yale Studies in English, 44. New York: H. Holt and Company, 1912.

Busby, Olive Mary. *Studies in the Development of the Fool in the Elizabethan Drama.* London: Oxford University Press, 1923.

Byrne, M. St. Clare. "Bibliographical Clues in Collaborate Plays," *Library,* 4th ser., 13 (1932), 21-48.

Cambridge History of English Literature. Edited by A.W. Ward and A.R. Waller. 15 vols. Cambridge: Cambridge University Press, 1932.

Canter, Howard Vernon. *Rhetorical Elements in the Tragedies of Seneca.* Vol. 10, no. 1 of the University of Illinois Studies in Language and Literature. Urbana: University of Illinois Press, 1925.

Cantrell, Paul L. and G.W. Williams. "The Printing of the Second Quarto of *Romeo and Juliet* (1599)," *Studies in Bibliography,* 9 (1957), 107-116.

Case, Shirley Jackson. *Makers of Christianity From Jesus to Charlemagne*. Reprint of the 1934 edition. Port Washington, New York: Kennikat Press, 1971.

Chambers, Edmund Kerchever. *The Elizabethan Stage*. 4 vols. Oxford: Clarendon Press, 1923.

Chappell, William, ed. *Old English Popular Music*. A new edition with a preface and notes, and the earlier examples entirely revised by H. Ellis Woolridge. London: Chappell, 1893.

Clemen, Wolfgang. *A Commentary on Shakespeare's Richard III*. Translated by Jean Bonheim. London: Methuen, 1968.

──────────. *English Tragedy Before Shakespeare*. Translated by T.S. Dorsch. London: Methuen, 1961.

──────────. "Shakespeare and Marlowe," *Shakespeare 1971*, ed. Clifford Leech and J.M.R. Margeson. Toronto: University of Toronto Press, 1972.

──────────. "Tradition and Originality in Shakespeare's *Richard III*," *Shakespeare Quarterly*, 5 (1954), 247-257.

Collier, John Payne. *A Bibliographical and Critical Account of the Rarest Books in the English Language*. 2 vols. London: Joseph Lilly, 1865.

Cousins, Frank W. *The Solar System*. London: John Baker, 1972.

Craig, Hardin. "Morality Plays and Elizabethan Drama," *Shakespeare Quarterly*, 1 (1950), 64-72.

──────────. "Revised Elizabethan Quartos: An Attempt to Form a Class," *Studies in the English Renaissance Drama in Memory of Karl Julius Holzknecht*, ed. Josephine W. Bennett, Oscar Cargill and Vernon Hall, Jr. New York: New York University Press, 1959.

──────────. "Shakespeare and the History Play," *Joseph Quincy Adams Memorial Studies*, ed. James G. McManaway, Giles E. Dawson and Edwin E. Willoughby. Washington: The Folger Shakespeare Library, 1948.

──────────. "The Shackling of Accidents: A Study of Elizabethan Tragedy," *Philological Quarterly*, 19 (1940), 1-19.

Crawford, Charles. "Edmund Spenser, 'Locrine' and 'Selimus'," *Notes and Queries*, 9th ser., 7 (1901), 61-63, 101-103, 142-144, 203-205, 261-263, 324-325, 384-386.

Creizenach, Wilhelm. *The English Drama in the Age of Shakespeare*. Translated from *Geschichte des neueren dramas*. London: Sidgwick & Jackson, 1916.

Cunliffe, John William. *Influence of Seneca on Elizabethan Tragedy*. London: Macmillan, 1893.

Cunningham, James Vincent. *Woe or Wonder; the Emotional Effect of Shakespearean Tragedy.* Denver: University of Denver Press, 1951.

Daniel, P.A. Letter to *The Athenaeum*, April 16, 1898, p. 512.

Dawson, Giles E. "Robert Walker's Editions of Shakespeare," *Studies in the English Renaissance Drama in Memory of Karl Julius Holzknecht*, ed. Josephine W. Bennett, Oscar Cargill and Vernon Hall, Jr. New York: New York University Press, 1959.

Doran, Madeleine. "Elements in the Composition of *King Lear*," *Studies in Philology*, 30 (1933), 34-58.

_____. *Endeavors of Art: A Study of Form in Elizabethan Drama.* Madison: University of Wisconsin Press, 1954.

Dowling, Harold M. "Peele and Some Doubtful Plays," *Notes & Queries*, 164 (1933), 366-370.

Draper, John W. "Falstaff, 'A Fool and Jester'," *Modern Language Quarterly*, 7 (1946), 453-462.

_____. *Stratford to Dogberry; Studies in Shakespeare's Earlier Plays.* Pittsburgh: University of Pittsburgh Press, 1961.

Eccles, Mark. "Chapman's Early Years," *Studies in Philology*, 43 (1946), 176-193.

_____. "Sir George Buc, Master of the Revels," *Thomas Lodge and Other Elizabethans*, ed. Charles J. Sisson. New York: Octagon Books, 1966.

Empson, William. *Some Versions of Pastoral.* London: Chatto & Windus, 1935.

Encyclopedia of the Classical World. Translated from Dutch by J. Muller-Van Santen, with emendations by Claire Jones. Englewood Cliffs, N.J.: Prentice-Hall, 1965.

Erbe, Theodor. "Die Locrinesage und die Quellen des pseudoshakespeareschen *Locrine*," *Studien zur englischen Philologie*, 16 (1904), 1-73.

Farmer, John S. and W.E. Henley, ed. *Slang and Its Analogues Past and Present.* 7 vols. London: Printed for Subscribers Only, 1890-1904.

Farnham, Willard. "John Higgins' *Mirror* and *Locrine*," *Modern Philology*, 23 (1925-26), 307-313.

Ferguson, Arthur B. *The Indian Summer of English Chivalry.* Durham, N.C.: Duke University Press, 1960.

Fleay, Frederick G. *A Biographical Chronicle of the English Drama 1559-1642.* 2 vols. London: Reeves and Turner, 1891.

Fogel, Ephim G. "Electronic Computers and Elizabethan Texts," *Studies in Bibliography*, 15 (1962), 15-31.

Foster, Francis A. "Dumb Show in Elizabethan Drama Before 1620," *Englische Studien*, 44 (1911), 8-17.

Freeman, Arthur. *Thomas Kyd.* Oxford: Clarendon Press, 1967.

_____. "Two Notes on *A Knack to Know a Knave*," *Notes & Queries*, n.s., 9 (1962), 326-327.

Freeman, Rosemary. *English Emblem Books.* London: Chatto & Windus, 1948.

Gaud, W.S. "The Authorship of *Locrine*," *Modern Philology*, 1 (1904), 409-422.

Gerrard, Ernest A. *Elizabethan Drama and Dramatists, 1583-1603.* Oxford: Oxford University Press, 1928.

Gibson, Harry Norman. *The Shakespeare Claimants.* London: Methuen, 1962.

Gilbert, A.H. "Seneca and the Criticism of Elizabethan Tragedy," *Philological Quarterly*, 13 (1934), 370-381.

Grant, Michael. *Myths of the Greeks and Romans.* Toronto: New American Library of Canada, 1962.

Graves, Robert. *The Greek Myths.* 2 vols. London: Penguin, 1955.

Graves, T.S. "The Authorship of 'Locrine'," *Times Literary Supplement*, January 8, 1925, p. 24.

Gray, Henry David. "Greene as a Collaborator," *Modern Language Notes*, 30 (1915), 244-246.

Greenfield, Thelma N. *The Induction in Elizabethan Drama.* Eugene: University of Oregon Books, 1969.

Greenlaw, Edwin. *Studies in Spenser's Historical Allegory.* Baltimore: The Johns Hopkins Press, 1932.

Greg, Walter W. "Authorship Attributions in the Play-Lists, 1656-1671," *Edinburgh Bibliographical Society Transactions*, 2 (1938-48), 303-329.

_____. *Principles of Emendation in Shakespeare.* London: H. Milford, 1928.

_____. "Review of Shakespere Forgeries," *Review of English Studies*, 5 (1929), 344-358.

Greg, Walter W. *The Shakespeare First Folio*. Oxford: Clarendon Press, 1955.

_____. "Three Manuscript Notes by Sir George Buc," *Library*, 4th ser., 12 (1932), 307-321.

Harbage, Alfred. "Elizabethan Acting," *Publications of the Modern Language Association*, 54 (1939), 685-708.

_____. *Shakespeare and the Rival Traditions*. New York: Macmillan, 1952.

Harper, Carrie A. "'Locrine' and the 'Faerie Queene'," *Modern Language Review*, 8 (1913), 369-371.

_____. *The Sources of British Chronicle History in Spenser's 'Faerie Queene'*. New York: Haskell House, 1964.

Harrison, G.B. *An Elizabethan Journal...1591-1594*. London: Constable, 1928.

Hart, Alfred. *Stolne and Surreptitious Copies, a Comparative Study of Shakespeare's Bad Quartos*. Melbourne and London: Melbourne University Press in association with Oxford University Press, 1942.

Heninger, S.K. "The Tudor Myth of Troy-novant," *South Atlantic Review*, 61 (1962), 378-387.

Herrick, Marvin T. "The Senecan Influence in *Gorboduc*," *Studies in Speech and Drama, in Honour of Alexander M. Drummond*. Ithaca: Cornell University Press, 1944, 78-104.

Hickson, Samuel. "Marlowe and the Old 'Taming of a Shrew'," *Notes & Queries*, 1st ser., 1 (1850), 194.

Hill, R.F. "Shakespeare's Early Tragic Mode," *Shakespeare Quarterly*, 9 (1958), 455-469.

Hoffman, Calvin. *The Murder of the Man Who Was 'Shakespeare'*. New York: Julian Messner, 1955.

Hoffmann, Gerhard. "Wandlungen des Gebets im elisabethanischen Drama," *Shakespeare-Jahrbuch* (Heidelberg), 102 (1966), 173-210.

Holmes, Elizabeth. *Aspects of Elizabethan Imagery*. Oxford: B. Blackwell, 1929.

Hubbard, Frank G. "A Type of Blank Verse Line Found in the Earlier Elizabethan Drama," *Publications of the Modern Language Association*, 32 (1917), 68-80.

_____. "*Locrine* and *Selimus*," *Shakespeare Studies* by Members of the Department of English in The University of Wisconsin. Madison: University of Wisconsin Press, 1916.

Hubbard, Frank G. "Repetition and Parallelism in the Earlier Elizabethan Drama," *Publications of the Modern Language Association*, 20 (1905), 360-379.

Hunter, G. K. "Review of *Studies in the Shakespeare Apocrypha*," *Modern Language Review*, 52 (1957), 587-588.

Hutson, A. E. *British Personal Names in the Historia Regum Britanniae*. Berkeley: University of California Press, 1940.

Jewkes, Wilfred T. *Act Division in Elizabethan and Jacobean Plays 1583-1616*. Hamden, Conn.: Shoe String Press, 1958.

Jordan, John Clark. *Robert Greene*. New York: Columbia University Press, 1915.

Jorgensen, Paul A. *Shakespeare's Military World*. Berkeley: University of California Press, 1956.

Joseph, Bertram Leon. *Elizabethan Acting*. London: Oxford University Press, 1951.

Joseph, Sister Miriam. *Shakespeare's Use of the Arts of Language*. New York: Hafner Publishing, 1966.

Kennedy, Milton Boone. *The Oration in Shakespeare*. Chapel Hill: University of North Carolina Press, 1942.

Kirschbaum, Leo. *Shakespeare and the Stationers*. Columbus: Ohio State University Press, 1955.

Knight, Charles, ed. *The Works of Shakspere*. New York: Virtue & Yorston, 1875-76.

Kökeritz, Helge. *Shakespeare's Pronunciation*. New Haven: Yale University Press, 1953.

Korninger, Siegfried. "Die Geisterszene im elisabethanischen Drama," *Shakespeare-Jahrbuch* (Heidelberg), 102 (1966), 124-145.

Langsam, G. Geoffrey. *Martial Books and Tudor Verse*. New York: King's Crown Press, 1951.

Larsen, Thorleif. "The Canon of Peele's Works," *Modern Philology*, 26 (1928), 191-199.

Lawrence, William J. *Pre-Restoration Stage Studies*. Cambridge, Massachusetts: Harvard University Press, 1927.

_____. *Shakespeare's Workshop*. Oxford: B. Blackwell, 1928.

Lea, Kathleen Marguerite. *Italian Popular Comedy; a Study in the Commedia Dell' Arte, 1560-1620, with Special Reference to the English Stage*. 2 vols. Oxford: Clarendon Press, 1934.

Levin, Richard. *The Multiple Plot in English Renaissance Drama.* Chicago: University of Chicago Press, 1971.

Lindabury, R.V. *A Study of Patriotism in the Elizabethan Drama.* Princeton: Princeton University Press, 1931.

Lotspeich, Henry Gibbons. *Classical Mythology in the Poetry of Edmund Spenser.* New York: Octagon Books, 1965.

Lucas, Frank Laurence. *Seneca and Elizabethan Tragedy.* Cambridge: Cambridge University Press, 1922.

Lyman, Dean B., Jr. "Apocryphal Plays of the University Wits," *English Studies in Honor of James Southall Wilson*, ed. Fredson Bowers. University of Virginia Studies, V. Charlottesville: University of Virginia, 1951.

Manly, J.M. "The Miracle Play in Mediaeval England," *Essays by Divers Hands; being the Transactions of the Royal Society of Literature of the United Kingdom*, 3rd ser., 7 (1927), 133-153.

Margeson, J.M.R. *The Origins of English Tragedy.* Oxford: Clarendon Press, 1967.

Maxwell, Baldwin. *Studies in the Shakespeare Apocrypha.* New York: King's Crown Press, 1956.

Maxwell, J.C. "Peele and Shakespeare: A Stylometric Test," *Journal of English and Germanic Philology*, 49 (1950), 557-61.

McDiarmid, Matthew P. "The Influence of Robert Garnier on Some Elizabethan Tragedies," *Etudes Anglaises*, 11 (1958), 289-302.

McIlwraith, A.K. "Marginalia on Press-Corrections," *Library*, 5th ser., 4 (1950), 238-248.

McKenzie, Donald F. "Printers of the Mind: Some Notes on Bibliographical Theories and Printing-House Practices," *Studies in Bibliography*, 22 (1969), 1-75.

McKerrow, Ronald Brunlees, ed. *A Dictionary of Printers and Booksellers in England, Scotland and Ireland, and of Foreign Printers of English Books 1557-1640.* London: Blades, East & Blades, 1910.

_____. *An Introduction to Bibliography for Literary Students.* Oxford: Clarendon Press, 1927.

_____. "Notes on Bibliographical Evidence for Literary Students and Editors of English Works of the Sixteenth and Seventeenth Centuries," *Transactions of the Bibliographical Society*, 12 (1914), 211-318.

_____. *Printers' & Publishers' Devices in England & Scotland 1485-1640.* London: Chiswick Press, 1913.

McKerrow, Ronald Brunlees. "The Elizabethan Printer and Dramatic Manuscripts," *Library*, 4th ser., 12 (1931), 253-275.

McManaway, James G. "Latin Title-Page Mottoes as a Clue to Dramatic Authorship," *Library*, 4th ser., 26 (1946), 28-36.

Mehl, Dieter. *The Elizabethan Dumb Show*. London: Methuen, 1965.

Monaghan, James. "Falstaff and His Forebears," *Studies in Philology*, 18 (1923), 353-361.

Moore, John Brooks. *The Comic and the Realistic in English Drama*. New York: Russell & Russell, 1965.

Moore, John Robert. "The Songs of the Public Theatres in the Time of Shakespeare," *Journal of English and Germanic Philology*, 28 (1929), 166-202.

Moorman, W.F. "The Pre-Shakespearian Ghost," *Modern Language Review*, 1 (1906), 85-95.

Muir, Kenneth. "*Locrine* and *Selimus*," *Times Literary Supplement*, August 12, 1944, p. 391.

_____. "Robert Greene as Dramatist," *Essays on Shakespeare and Elizabethan Drama in Honor of Hardin Craig*, ed. Richard Hosley. Columbia: University of Missouri Press, 1962.

_____. *Shakespeare as Collaborator*. London: Methuen, 1960.

Murray, John Tucker. *English Dramatic Companies, 1558-1642*. 2 vols. New York: Russell & Russell, 1963.

Naylor, E.W. *Shakespeare and Music*. London: Dent, 1931.

New Century Classical Handbook, The. Edited by Catherine B. Avery. New York: Appleton-Century-Crofts, 1962.

Nichols, John. *The Progresses and Public Processions of Queen Elizabeth...* 3 vols. London: John Nichols and Son, 1823.

_____. *The Progresses, Processions, and Magnificent Festivities of King James the First...* 4 vols. London: J.B. Nichols, 1828.

Ogburn, Dorothy and Charlton. *This Star of England*. New York: Coward-McCann, 1952.

Onions, Charles Talbut. *A Shakespeare Glossary*. Oxford: Clarendon Press, 1911.

Oxford Classical Dictionary, The. Edited by N.G.L. Hammond and H.H. Scullard. 2nd ed. Oxford: Clarendon Press, 1970.

Oxford Dictionary of English Proverbs. Compiled by William George Smith with introduction and index by Janet E. Heseltine. Oxford: Clarendon Press, 1948.

Oxford English Dictionary, The. Edited by James A.H. Murray, Henry Bradley, W.A. Craigie, C.T. Onions. Oxford: Clarendon Press, 1933.

Palmer, D.J. "Elizabethan Tragic Heroes," *Elizabethan Theatre, Stratford-Upon-Avon Studies,* 9 (1966), 10-35.

Parks, Edd Winfield. "Simms Edition of the Shakespeare Apocrypha," *Studies in Shakespeare,* ed. Arthur D. Matthews and Clark M. Emery. Coral Gables, Florida: University of Miami Press, 1953.

Parsons, A.E. "The Trojan Legend in England," *Modern Language Review,* 24 (1929), 253-264, 394-408.

Partridge, Astley Cooper. *Orthography in Shakespeare and Elizabethan Drama.* London: E. Arnold, 1964.

Partridge, Edward B. *The Broken Compass: A Study of the Major Comedies of Ben Jonson.* London: Chatto & Windus, 1958.

Partridge, Eric. *Shakespeare's Bawdy: A Literary & Psychological Essay and a Comprehensive Glossary.* London: Routledge & Kegan Paul, 1968.

Paterson, Morton. "The Stagecraft of the Revels Office During the Reign of Elizabeth," *Studies in the Elizabethan Theatre,* ed. C.T. Prouty. New Haven: Shoe String Press, 1961.

Pearn, B.R. "Dumb Show in Elizabethan Drama," *Review of English Studies,* 11 (1935), 385-405.

Pinciss, G.M. "Thomas Creede and the Repertory of the Queen's Men, 1583-1592," *Modern Philology,* 67 (1970), 321-330.

Pitcher, Seymour Maitland. *The Case for Shakespeare's Authorship of The Famous Victories.* New York: State University of New York, 1961.

Plomer, H.R. "The Printers of Shakespeare's Plays and Poems," *Library,* 2nd ser., 7 (1906), 149-167.

Pollard, Alfred W. "Elizabethan Spelling as a Literary and Bibliographical Clue," *Library,* 4th ser., 4 (1923), 1-8.

Pope, Alexander. "Preface to the Works of Shakespear," *The Works of Alexander Pope, Esq. in Verse and Prose,* ed. Rev. William Lisle Bowles. 10 vols. London, 1806.

Povey, K. "Variant Formes in Elizabethan Printing," *Library,* 5th ser., 10 (1955), 41-48.

Praz, Mario. "Machiavelli and the Elizabethans," *Proceedings of the British Academy*, 14 (1928), 49-97.

Predecessors of Shakespeare, The. A Survey and Bibliography of Recent Studies in English Renaissance Drama. Edited by Terence P. Logan and Denzell S. Smith. Lincoln: University of Nebraska Press, 1973.

Prior, Moody E. "Imagery as a Test of Authorship," *Shakespeare Quarterly*, 6 (1955), 381-386.

Reed, Robert Rentoul, Jr. *The Occult on the Tudor and Stuart Stage.* Boston: Christopher Publishing House, 1965.

Reese, Max M. *The Cease of Majesty; A Study of Shakespeare's History Plays.* London: E. Arnold, 1961.

Ribner, Irving. "Greene's Attack on Marlowe; Some Light on *Alphonsus* and *Selimus*," *Studies in Philology*, 52 (1955), 162-171.

_____. "Morality Roots of the Tudor History Play," *Tulane Studies in English*, 4 (1954), 21-43.

_____. *Patterns in Shakespearian Tragedy.* London: Methuen, 1960.

_____. *The English History Play in the Age of Shakespeare.* Princeton: Princeton University Press, 1957.

Riggs, David. *Shakespeare's Heroical Histories.* Cambridge, Massachusetts: Harvard University Press, 1971.

Righter, Anne. *Shakespeare and the Idea of the Play.* London: Chatto & Windus, 1962.

Robertson, John Mackinnon. *Did Shakespeare Write "Titus Andronicus"?* London: Watts, 1905.

Rosenberg, Marvin. "Elizabethan Actors: Men or Marionettes?" *Publications of the Modern Language Association*, 69 (1954), 915-927.

Rossiter, A.P. *English Drama From Early Times to the Elizabethans.* London: Hutchinson University Library, 1950.

Sampley, A.M. "Plot Structure in Peele's Plays as a Test of Authorship," *Publications of the Modern Language Association*, 51 (1936), 689-701.

_____. "'Verbal Tests' for Peele's Plays," *Studies in Philology*, 30 (1933), 473-496.

Schelling, Felix Emmanuel. *Elizabethan Drama, 1558-1642.* 2 vols. London: Constable, 1908.

Schelling, Felix Emmanuel. *Foreign Influences in Elizabethan Plays*. London: Harper & Brothers Publishers, 1923.

_____. *The English Chronicle Play*. London: Macmillan, 1902.

Schlegel, August Wilhelm. *A Course of Lectures on Dramatic Art and Literature*. Translated by John Black. London: Bell, 1846.

Schoeck, Richard J., ed. *Editing Sixteenth Century Texts*. Toronto: University of Toronto Press, 1966.

Schoenbaum, Samuel. *Annals of English Drama 975-1700; A Second Supplement to the Revised Edition*. Evanston: Northwestern University Press, 1970.

_____. *Internal Evidence and Elizabethan Dramatic Authorship*. Evanston: Northwestern University Press, 1966.

Shaaber, M.A. "Review of *Studies in the Shakespeare Apocrypha*," *Modern Language Notes*, 72 (1957), 290-292.

_____. "The Meaning of the Imprint in Early Printed Books," *Library*, 4th ser., 24 (1944), 132-133.

Simpson, Richard. "Review of Wolfgang Bernhardi's *Robert Greene's Leben und Schriften*," *The Academy*, March 21, 1874, p. 310.

_____. *Shakespere Allusion-Books*. London: N. Trübner, 1874.

Smith, Grover. "The Tennis-Ball of Fortune," *Notes & Queries*, 16th ser., 190 (1946), 202-203.

Spencer, Theodore. *Death and Elizabethan Tragedy*. Cambridge, Massachusetts: Harvard University Press, 1936.

Spivey, Gaynell Callaway. "Swinburne's Use of Elizabethan Drama," *Studies in Philology*, 41 (1944), 250-263.

Spurgeon, Caroline F.E. *Shakespeare's Imagery and What It Tells Us*. Cambridge: Cambridge University Press, 1935.

Stamp, A.E. *The Disputed Revels Accounts*. London: Oxford University Press, 1930.

Starnes, De Witt Talmage and Ernest William Talbert. *Classical Myth and Legend in Renaissance Dictionaries*. Chapel Hill: University of North Carolina Press, 1955.

Starnes, De Witt Talmage. "Richard Taverner's *The Garden of Wisdom*, Carion's Chronicles, and the Cambyses Legend," *University of Texas Studies in English*, 35 (1956), 22-31.

Symonds, John A. *Shakespeare's Predecessors in the English Drama.* London: Smith, Elder, 1900.

Talbert, Ernest William. *Elizabethan Drama and Shakespeare's Early Plays.* Chapel Hill: University of North Carolina Press, 1963.

Tannenbaum, Samuel Aaron. *Shakspere Forgeries in the Revels Accounts.* Port Washington, New York: Kennikat Press, 1966.

_____. *Shaksperian Scraps and Other Elizabethan Fragments.* New York: Columbia University Press, 1933.

Tatlock, John Strong Perry. *The Legendary History of Britain: Geoffrey of Monmouth's Historia Regum Britanniae and its Early Vernacular Versions.* Berkeley: University of California Press, 1950.

Taylor, Rupert. "A Tentative Chronology of Marlowe's and Some Other Elizabethan Plays," *Publications of the Modern Language Association*, 51 (1936), 643-688.

Thorp, Willard. *The Triumph of Realism in Elizabethan Drama, 1558-1612.* New York: Haskell House, 1965.

Thorpe, James. *Principles of Textual Criticism.* San Marino: The Huntington Library, 1972.

Tilley, Morris Palmer. *A Dictionary of the Proverbs in England in the Sixteenth and Seventeenth Centuries.* Ann Arbor: University of Michigan Press, 1950.

Tillyard, E.M.W. *Elizabethan World Picture.* London: Chatto & Windus, 1943.

Turner, Robert Y. "Shakespeare and the Public Confrontation Scene in Early History Plays," *Modern Philology*, 62 (1964), 1-12.

Ulrici, Hermann. *Shakespeare's Dramatic Art.* London: Chapman Brothers, 1846.

Venezky, Alice Sylvia. *Pageantry on the Shakespearian Stage.* New York: Twayne Publishers, 1951.

Vickers, Brian. *The Artistry of Shakespeare's Prose.* London: Methuen, 1968.

Ward, Sir Aldolphus W. *A History of English Dramatic Literature to the Death of Queen Anne.* 3 vols. London and New York: Macmillan, 1899.

Watson, Sara R. "'Gorboduc' and the Theory of Tyrannicide," *Modern Language Review*, 34 (1939), 355-366.

Wells, Stanley. *Modernizing Shakespeare's Spelling.* Published with Gary Taylor, *Three Studies in the Text of Henry V.* Oxford: Clarendon Press, 1979.

Welsford, Enid. *The Fool: His Social and Literary History*. Garden City, New York: Doubleday, 1961.

Who's Who in the Theatre. Edited by Freda Gaye. Fourteenth Edition. London: Sir Isaac Pitman & Sons, 1967.

Wickham, Glynne W.G. *Early English Stages, 1300-1600*. 3 vols. London: Routledge and Kegan Paul, 1959.

Williams, George Walton. "The Good Quarto of *Romeo and Juliet*, A Bibliographical Study." Ph.D. dissertation, University of Virginia, 1957.

Wilson, F.P. *Marlowe and the Early Shakespeare*. Oxford: Clarendon Press, 1953.

_____. *Shakespeare and the New Bibliography*. Revised and edited by Helen Gardner. Oxford: Clarendon Press, 1970.

Winslow, Ola Elizabeth. *Low Comedy as a Structural Element in English Drama from the Beginnings to 1642*. Chicago: University of Chicago Libraries, 1926.

Wright, Joseph, ed. *The English Dialect Dictionary,...* 6 vols. London: H. Frowde, 1898-.

Wright, Louis B. "Heywood and the Popularizing of History," *Modern Language Notes*, 43 (1928), 287-293.

Glossarial Index to the Commentary

This index, following the pattern set out in *The Revels Plays* (published by Manchester University Press and The Johns Hopkins University Press), lists only those words, names, and phrases (including proverbs) which have been explained in the commentary. However, certain types of annotations do not appear: the numerous parallel passages between *Locrine* and other contemporary works, discussions of textual readings, translations of Latin, rhetorical devices, explanations of stage directions and stage business, and comments about character or theme. Words and phrases appear as they do in the text of the play with the exception of plural nouns, which are normally cited in the singular, and tenses of verbs, which are cited in the infinitive. Phrases are listed under their key words. Most entries give only one line reference, indicating that the first use of the term establishes its meaning in the play; further references (if any) are not noted. Two line references beside an entry indicate that the term has been used in two different senses in the play.

Abis,II,vii,25
abominable,II,iv,53
abroach,II,v,18;V,vi,198
Aby,IV,v,31
Abyssus,IV,v,18
accident,III,ii,42;III,iii,53
Acheron,IV,iii,63
aconitum,IV,iii,8
acquittance,V,v,66
adament,III,v,7
Aeacus,I,ii,235
affection,V,v,48
agnominate,III,iii,4
Albania,III,ii,88
Albion,I,ii,116
Alcmena,III,v,35
Alecto,IV,iii,5
aliquant,I,iii,28
amain,II,iii,33;III,ii,40
ambrosia,II,vii,22
Amphion,III,ii,9
an,IV,iii,85
Andromeda,II,i,2
annoy,*sb*.,II,iii,37

Antastick,I,iii,2
Anthropophagi,III,vii,34
Antigonus,I,ii,95
apple of mine eye,V,iii,32
Aquitaine,I,ii,49
arcane,V,v,43
argent,III,v,14
Argive,III,v,9
as,II,ii,80
Assaracus,I,ii,88
at a bit,IV,iii,36
Ate,I,i,0.1
Aurora,I,ii,52
Avernus,IV,v,19

Bablatrice,II,vi,101
backside,II,iv,82
bale, work thy,I,iii,20
balls, tennis,II,vi,18
ban,*vb*,III,vii,8
barking dog...strangers bite,IV, ii,120
bastinado,II,iii,62
bear out,I,ii,214

167

168   TRAGEDY OF LOCRINE

beardless boy,V,ii,45
bees have stings, shuns the
   hives...,III,iii,40
Bellerophon,I,ii,37
Bellona,III,v,4
benight,IV,iii,39
bewray,V,v,43
bird,V,v,8
bird-bolt,I,iii,14-15
bit, at a,IV,iii,36
blue hood,II,iii,70
bobekin,II,vi,114
bootless,V,iii,25
Boreas,II,i,57
boy, beardless,V,ii,45
braves, brook no,V,iv,14
Briareus,II,vi,7
brickbat,II,vi,99
Bridewell,III,iv,33
Brittany,I,iv,1
brook no braves,V,iv,14
buck,II,iv,64
bucking-tub,I,iii,11
burgonet,II,ii,84
buskin,II,iii,43
but,II,v,23
by dint of...sword,II,ii,66
by my dorth,III,iv,4
by our lady,II,iv,87

Caithness,II,iii,45
Caledon,II,iv,23
Cambria,III,ii,71
can,sb.,II,iii,17
canvasado,II,iii,62
cap, Scotch,IV,iii,20.1
capcase,I,iii,97
Caphareus,IV,ii,61
Capontail,II,iii,61
Captain,II,iv,70
carbuncle,IV,iv,26
career,II,iv,28
carouse,II,vii,21
cavalier,II,iv,1
Cepheus,II,i,3
Ceraunia,III,vii,30
Cerberus, triple,I,ii,76
Ceres,IV,iii,60
Chimaera,II,vi,54
chivalry,I,ii,51
chuff,V,iv,1
cipher,IV,ii,163
clock, what's a,IV,iii,50
clod,II,vii,23
closet,V,vi,139

clout,vb,II,iii,44
cockatrice,II,vi,101
cockscomb,II,v,20
Cocytus,III,vii,13
Codpiece...done thy master,III,
   iv,57
Codshead,III,iv,36
column,I,ii,145
commandments, ten,IV,iii,41
common-house,II,iii,82
company, for,II,iii,25
concourse,IV,ii,41
Constultations,I,iii,5
contagious foam,IV,iii,7
contentation,II,ii,35
contributory,I,ii,97
contrived,II,i,7
coraggio,IV,iii,24
coronet,II,ii,28;II,v,1
corpse,III,iii,28;V,vi,116
correspondent,I,ii,210
corsive,III,vii,37
Corus,I,ii,117
courser,II,iv,30
court it out,V,ii,109
cousin,I,ii,257
Cox,II,vi,114
crazèd,I,ii,221
crown,sb.,II,vi,27
Croydon,II,vi,107
Cuprit,I,iii,14
curious,IV,iv,22
curtle-axe,IV,ii,22
cut,vb,II,ii,8

Dacian,II,ii,6
dart,sb.,IV,iii,0.2
decent,IV,ii,93
defect,sb.,I,ii,216
Demogorgon,I,ii,233
detract the fight,III,v,52
Dina,I,iii,18
disannul,I,ii,34
dismal,I,i,11
distaff,IV,i,0.4
distill,V,vi,101
dite,I,iii,28
dorth, by my,III,iv,4
doubted,III,v,34
dram of joy...pound of care,
   IV,ii,102
draw,II,iii,61
dress,vb,III,iv,25
Durolitum,IV,iv,19

INDEX

Ecstasy,V,ii,42
eftsoons,IV,iv,31
Elysian fields,I,ii,226
eme,I,ii,88
end, unto his,I,ii,140
enterprise,*vb*,I,ii,74
entertainment,II,ii,68
Eos,II,ii,96
equalize,IV,ii,5
Erebus,I,ii,244
Erinnys,III,vii,21
erst,III,iii,57
Euripus,IV,v,13
Eurus,II,ii,45
excrement,IV,v,5
expect,I,ii,248
eye, apple of mine,V,iii,32

Famés,IV,iii,9
fatal sisters,I,ii,38
Fates,I,ii,33
fear,*vb*,I,ii,236
fere,V,v,49
fetch,II,iv,28
field, pitchèd,I,ii,96
fight, detract the,III,v,52
figured,I,iv,13
firmament,III,v,33
flakes, icy,II,vi,57
Flora,II,ii,33
foam, contagious,IV,iii,7
foil, sustain the,I,ii,112
for,I,ii,149
for company,II,iii,25
forager,II,iv,94
fox, I smell a,II,vi,93
frame,I,iii,66
fraught,IV,iv,22
front,II,vi,12;V,vi,37
froward,V,iii,50;V,vi,110
frump,V,v,58
furnish up,II,ii,107

Gathelus,I,ii,111
glaive,V,vi,88
glass,I,ii,224
Goffarius,I,ii,48
Gogmagog,I,ii,119
gog's,II,iii,70
guardiant,I,ii,53

Habitacle,II,iv,52
halidom,II,iii,71
halter,III,iv,56
happy isles,II,ii,49

haste, the more, the worst speed, I,iii,33
haw,IV,v,4
Hebe,I,ii,85
Hecate, triple,V,i,6
Hecuba,III,ii,48;IV,ii,61-65
hem with,III,v,3
Hercules,III,ii,16;III,v,35
'hest,I,ii,142
his,II,vi,10;III,iii,20
hogshead,I,iii,12
honeycomb, He is not worthy..., III,iii,39
hood, blue,II,iii,66
hugie,I,ii,238
Hydra,III,ii,17

I smell a fox,II,vi,92-93
Icarus,I,ii,36
icy flake,II,vi,57
Illyrian sea,I,ii,108
implement,II,iii,64
incontinent,V,iv,5
ingeny,I,ii,73
Innogen,I,ii,199
Iscan,III,ii,72
isles, happy,II,ii,49
Ixion,III,vii,46

Jacinth,III,v,31
just,III,ii,67

Knaves trumps,IV,iii,40

Labres, succado de,I,iii,98
Lactantius,I,iii,5
ladies, learned nine,II,ii,40
lady, by our,II,iv,87
lady, watery,V,v,17
latest,IV,ii,173
leese,V,ii,64
Lestrigon,I,ii,105
Lethe,III,vii,15
letter,I,iii,68
Limbo,III,vii,51
lobcock,III,iv,26
losel,V,ii,71
Lucifer,II,ii,81
lure,I,ii,184
Lynceus,IV,iv,17

Macerate,V,ii,33
make,III,iii,54
map,*sb*.,V,vi,73
Mass,III,iv,17

masty,V,vi,170
mate,III,ii,23
maugre,II,ii,18
mavortial,IV,ii,52
maze, a,V,vi,0.4
me, say,III,ii,18
meat,IV,iii,4
Mercia,V,i,16
Mercury,II,iv,61;IV,iii,75
Meroe,II,vi,48
million,II,ii,64
mind, youngest in,I,ii,207
Minerva,II,vi,11
Minos,I,ii,251
mirror,sb.,IV,i,3
mischief follows...neck,V,vi, 176
Molossian,I,ii,47
Monichus,II,vi,9
mood,II,vi,3;IV,ii,55
Mors,I,ii,246
mother,IV,iv,12
mungrel,III,ii,3
muses, nine,II,ii,40
Myrmidon,III,ii,46

Nactaball,II,iii,59
nappy,II,iii,17
Nicebice,III,iv,31
nine muses,II,ii,40
Niobe,III,ii,54
no will,II,iii,64
noise,I,ii,241
note, turn his,II,iii,40
novelty,II,ii,61

Oak, sacred,I,ii,25
occision,IV,ii,4
Ocean,I,ii,3
ophirs,IV,iv,25
Orpheus,III,ii,5
out, bear,I,ii,214
out, court it,V,ii,109
outrageous,III,vii,28

Pallas,V,vi,79
Pandrassus,I,ii,46
pantofle,IV,i,0.4
'parel,I,iii,42
pasteboard,II,iii,61
pate,I,iii,27
Pelops,I,ii,248
Penthesilea,II,ii,90
Pergamus,III,ii,49
Perseus,II,i,2

petty treason,II,iv,81
Phineus,II,i,6
Phoebus,II,ii,40
Phrygian,II,ii,9
pigsney,I,iii,72
pillowbear,IV,v,6
pitchèd field,I,ii,96
pittering,II,ii,46
plackets,III,iv,58
planets, seven,I,iii,1
platform,IV,ii,51
plaudite,V,vi,84
Pluto,I,ii,245
policy,II,v,8
Polycrates,II,iv,37
Polyphemus,III,vii,33
portion,IV,iii,48
Posthumius,II,ii,10
pound of care, dram of joy..., IV,ii,102
prejudicating,V,v,3
premise,V,vi,199
press,vb,II,iii,39
press-money,II,iii,47
pretence,V,v,39
prevent,V,vi,118
princox,II,v,21
process,IV,i,16
Prometheus,III,vii,47
proper,I,ii,16
pudding-time,III,iv,24
pull,vb,II,iii,27
Puryflegiton,III,vii,18
Pyrrhus,III,ii,52

'Quite,IV,ii,157

Reave,II,vi,82
reclaim,V,iii,40
redoubted,III,ii,4
regiment,III,ii,66
rent,I,ii,78
reproachful,V,iii,48
retire,II,v,6
Rhamnus,II,ii,20
Rhamnusia,II,vii,2
Risus,I,iv,14
roseal,IV,ii,92
Roydon,II,vi,107
runagate,II,iv,14

Sabren,V,iv,0.1
sacred oak,I,ii,25
Satyri,V,vi,137
saucebox,III,iv,26

INDEX

say me,III,ii,18
scathe,V,iii,33
Scotch cap,IV,iii,20.1
scouring,IV,iii,23
screaking,II,vi,105
scripture,I,iii,30
Scythian,II,i,14
Semeleius,II,vii,24
Semiramis,II,ii,74
sempiternal,I,ii,155
sentences, vulgar,IV,ii,138
seven planets,I,iii,1
shamble,II,vi,103
shuns the hives...bees have stings,III,iii,40
Signior,I,iii,49
silly,I,i,8
Simois,II,iv,33
sisters, fatal,I,ii,38
Sisyphus,III,iii,50
sith,II,vii,29
snail doth climb...tops, II,ii,1
sorted,I,ii,156
speed, the more haste the worst,I,iii,33
spin a fair thread,II,iii,84
squadrant,II,vi,5
squeltering,II,vii,4
squire,V,ii,55
state,II,iii,37
stayless,V,vi,108
stomach serve you,II,iii,70
stour,II,vi,111
straggling,III,ii,2
strangers bite, barking dog ...,IV,ii,120
strangle,I,ii,29
straw,III,iii,19
stream,*sb*.,III,v,14
stretch,II,iii,78
strike,I,i,12;V,ii,42
Stygian lake,III,vi,5
Styx,IV,v,16
suburb,II,iv,60
succado de labres,I,iii,98
superbious,II,v,25
suspire,V,v,2
sustain the foil,I,ii,112
sword, by dint of,II,ii,66
Sylvan,II,ii,46

Taenarus,IV,v,43
Tantalus,I,ii,248
target,II,i,0.4
Tartarus,I,ii,75
teeth, to the,V,v,33
Tellus,V,v,10
Tempe,II,ii,47
temperature,II,ii,31
ten commandments,IV,iii,41
tender,*vb*,I,ii,192
Tenedos,III,iii,58
tennis balls,II,vi,18
that,I,iv,2;III,v,36
Thessaly,II,ii,39
Thetis,III,iii,7
thrall,IV,ii,150
thread, spin a fair,II,iii,84
Tisiphone,I,ii,254
Titan,II,ii,95
Tithonus,I,ii,250
Tityus,V,vi,125
to the teeth,V,v,33
Tom,I,iii,18
torrid zone,IV,iii,58
town-house,II,iii,58
transfretting,I,ii,108
treason, petty,II,iv,81
trenchant,II,iv,2
triple Cerberus,I,ii,76
triple Hecate,V,i,6
triple world,V,v,5
Troglodyte,IV,ii,30
Trompart,I,iii,51
trophy,I,ii,44
Troynovant,I,ii,263
trumps, knaves,IV,iii,40
Trussier,II,v,0.1
tunny,II,vi,114
turn his note,II,iii,40
Turnus,I,ii,113

Uncouth,II,ii,61
unpartial,I,ii,23
unto his end,I,ii,140
up, furnish,II,ii,107
upshot,III,iii,45
use,*vb*,V,ii,73

Venerean,V,ii,55
vengible,I,iii,14
victory,I,ii,43
vindicta,III,vii,54
virent,III,iii,11
vulgar sentences,IV,ii,138

Warding,III,iii,54
warned when...young,III,iv,35
watery lady,V,v,17

wayment,II,iii,86
what's a clock,IV,iii,50
whereas,I,ii,106
will,*sb.*,V,iii,10
will, no,II,iii,69
within,IV,iii,42
withouten,II,iii,19
woody nymph,V,v,18
work thy bale,I,iii,20
world, triple,V,v,5
wrong,*adv.*,I,ii,65

Xanthus,III,v,9

Yard of land,IV,iii,48
youngest in mind,I,ii,205

Zone, torrid,IV,iii,55

LIBRARY OF DAVIDSON COLLEGE

may be checked out for **two weeks**.